D1171897

Assimilation and Association
in French Colonial Theory
1890–1914

NUMBER *604*
COLUMBIA STUDIES IN THE SOCIAL SCIENCES
EDITED BY THE FACULTY OF POLITICAL SCIENCE
OF COLUMBIA UNIVERSITY

AMS PRESS

NEW YORK

Assimilation and Association

in French Colonial Theory

1890-1914

RAYMOND F. BETTS

COLUMBIA UNIVERSITY PRESS

New York and London   1961

COLUMBIA UNIVERSITY
STUDIES IN THE
SOCIAL SCIENCES

604

Copyright © 1960 Columbia University Press
First published in book form 1961

The series was formerly known as
Studies in History, Economics and Public Law.

Reprinted from a copy in the collections of the
Brooklyn Public Library.

Reprinted with the permission of Columbia University Press
From the edition of 1961, New York
First AMS EDITION published 1970
Manufactured in the United States of America

Library of Congress Catalog Card Number: 70-130622

International Standard Book Number:
            Complete Set: 0-404-51000-0
            Number 604: 0-404-51604-1

AMS PRESS, INC.
New York, N. Y. 10003

TO MY MOTHER AND FATHER

PREFACE

THIS book considers an aspect of French colonial theory that was of particular importance in the formative years of the second French colonial empire. While all sorts of problems relating to the administration of the new empire perplexed Frenchmen, none was more acute or important than that of the relationship to be established with the native populations submitted to French control. Consideration of this problem led to a shift in theory from the idea of assimilation to the idea of association. Rather than attempt to absorb the native societies administratively and culturally into the French nation, France was to pursue a more flexible policy which would emphasize retention of local institutions and which would make the native an associate in the colonial enterprise. This is the essence of the ideas discussed by the theorists and popularizers in metropolitan France during the period under examination. The reasons for the shift comprise most of the chapter headings in this study.

Perhaps at no other period in French history was more active interest in colonial problems expressed by Frenchmen than that between 1890 and 1914. And yet the colonial theory discussed in metropolitan France during this time has not received the analysis it merits. The attention of students of French colonial history is usually turned away from France to the overseas possessions where the most dramatic action was taking place between the fall of the second ministry of Jules Ferry in 1885 and the holocaust of the First World War. There is, nonetheless, a need to show how French colonial theory was evolving at home in face of the complexities of modern colonial rule. I hope that this study fills this need in so far as the native problem is concerned.

My indebtedness is great and willingly expressed. I am grateful to Professor Robert D. Cross of Columbia University, who read the manuscript with the eye of an editor. And I wish to thank most warmly Professor Ambroise Jobert of the University of Grenoble, who gave me the benefits of that intelligent criticism which I like to believe characteristically French. The librarians of the Bibliothèque nationale and the Ecole nationale de la France d'outre-mer were generous with their assistance. The French Government saw fit to finance a trip to Africa which enabled me to see for myself a part of the colonial empire which had attracted my attention. I also wish to thank the editors of the *Cahiers d'histoire* for permission to use my article, "L'Influence des méthodes hollandaises et anglaises sur la doctrine coloniale française à la fin du XIXe siècle," in this essay.

To Professor Shepard B. Clough of Columbia University who so strongly aroused my interest in French history and who so patiently assisted me in studying its ways I happily and deeply express my thanks.

My wife Jackie has been a loving critic. Her New Hampshire common sense and her gentle patience were given to me when needed, as they always are.

RAYMOND F. BETTS

Havertown, Pennsylvania
April, 1961

CONTENTS

Assimilation and Association

in French Colonial Theory

1890–1914

Chapter 1

THE CLIMATE OF FRENCH COLONIALISM

POLITICALLY, France looks in two directions. Inward she sees the continent and the country of the Rhine where so many national dreams have been realized and so many shattered. Outward she views the waters of two seas which have carried Frenchmen, French ideas, and French goods to the regions of the world that bend beyond the horizon. Fewer dreams have been inspired by this view, but the history of French expansion overseas has an interest all its own.

In a way it is a curious history, for the French have never really had their heart in colonial activities. It has been said that the British Empire was acquired in a "fit of absence of mind," but no such remark has ever been made about the French Empire, amassed in the face of public apathy at best, antipathy at worst. Yet this did not prevent the French from constructing on two occasions an overseas empire second only to that of Great Britain.

The first of France's two empires disintegrated into near nothingness by the beginning of the nineteenth century. Britain, France's rival on the land as on the seas, saw to its reduction, but the French themselves were not gravely interested in its defense. Seldom torn between the two essential choices open to her in foreign policy, France was directed inland, toward the north and the east where her destiny seemed to lie. She was chiefly a continental power, despite her long coastlines. When the first colonial empire fell apart, the laments at home were not numerous.

After the Napoleonic epoch France was returned some of her old possessions, which then served as the first building blocks of a new and more imposing overseas empire. The acquisition of Algeria in 1830 really began the process which was sporadically continued throughout the century. However, the important construction of this empire dates from the Tunisian venture of 1881 and remains the work of the Third Republic.

The fact that the Third Republic's life runs a course parallel to that of the new overseas empire does not mean that the two shared the same heart. Had France lived under a different form of government after 1870, the phenomenon might still have occurred.

The rush overseas is a salient characteristic of the history of Europe in the last quarter of the nineteenth century. Almost every European nation of importance engaged in the activity, and all converged on the one area still open to intensive penetration, Africa. Although such expansion had occurred throughout the century, the keenness of the competition now enlarged the importance of the problem and made it vital to European and world affairs.

From the first the French were involved; the tricolor was planted in Asia as well as in Africa. Yet these doings were not loudly cheered by the populace at home. In fact,

French overseas expansion aroused little enthusiasm among the French people of the nineteenth century. Voltaire's famous quip about the worthlessness of Canada might well have found contemporary expression in the outbursts over Algeria, Indochina, or Tunisia, outbursts which punctuated otherwise long periods of governmental apathy toward expansion. During the early days of the Third Republic the handful of partisans of colonial expansion was constrained from doing any more than trying to justify this expansion to an often hostile parliament and to a disinterested populace.

In the vanguard was the deputy from the industrial region of the Vosges, the ardent republican, Jules Ferry. Ferry, premier in 1881 and again from 1883 to 1885, later popularized the chief arguments called forth to explain and justify the need for overseas expansion.[1] While he spoke of strategic needs and patriotic duty, he used arguments that were primarily economic and which were similarly stated in many countries of Europe. Glancing at the world about him, Ferry described the workings of the capitalist, industrial machine: keen economic competition, growing national protectionism expressed in tariff regulations. He acclaimed the overseas possessions as the outlets, the necessary markets, for French goods, and as places for the investment of capital. Colonial policy was the daughter of industrial policy, he stated, and in this brief expression is contained the essence of his colonial doctrine.

In reality the French people were not asked to initiate a policy of overseas expansion but rather to accept it. It is not too rash to state that the theories and suggestions of men like Ferry were but ex post facto justifications for an activity carried on by a handful of ambitious, roaming, or patriotic individuals who may even have cared little about the acute problems of late nineteenth-century capitalism.[2] In often haphazard fashion they staked out claims to areas hitherto hardly considered by the white man; sometimes they found themselves—if the pun will be excused—in a stew from which France had to retrieve them. France's overseas empire was largely acquired without plan or purpose, at least in so far as many Frenchmen could see.

Yet, beginning around 1890, the French imperialists found themselves in an atmosphere that was rather conducive to the development of colonial policy. The anticolonial spirit began to lessen. One of its most obvious causes, worry over France's weak continental position, was momentarily removed. The "blue line of the Vosges," watched with bitterness by the *revanchards,* was no longer so prominent. The alliance with Russia gave France some assurance of security in Europe. At least the denunciation of colonial expansion as an enterprise sapping vital continental military power now lost some of its potency.

At home the political opponents of empire began to give way. The rural population, isolationist and hence anticolonial, was satisfied by the finance law of 1900 which shifted the burden of empire so that direct aid to the colonies was stopped.[3] With Gabriel Hanotaux at the Quai d'Orsay in 1894, colonial expansion became an accepted part of foreign policy. Although bitter debates on colonial problems were still to be heard in the Chamber of Deputies, only the Socialists continued their ardent condemnation of imperialism,[4] and even within this particular group an individual as prominent as Jean Jaurès was able to find justifications for overseas expansion.[5]

Along with the obvious weakening of the anticolonial spirit, other important changes began to take place. In Paris the International Colonial Congress of 1889 and the National Colonial Congress of 1889–90 gave initial impetus to the new colonial movement. Then in rapid succession followed the founding of the Ecole coloniale in 1889, the return of the outstanding imperialist Eugène Etienne to the position of Undersecretary of State for Colonies in that same year, and the establishment in 1890 of the largest of French colonial societies, the Comité de l'Afrique française. Moreover, the exotic novels of Loti, Bertrand, and Farrère attracted a growing number of readers and directed their attention overseas, as did several periodicals devoted to the colonial cause.[6] And a number of colonial congresses held principally between the years 1900 and 1909 brought together those individuals in France who followed the colonial movement with keen appreciation.[7] Thus, in several ways the French public slowly awakened to the importance of the overseas empire.

At the center of all this activity was to be found a hard core of imperialists, a group generally labeled the "colonial party." These men, few in number, consolidated their efforts primarily through two agencies: the colonial societies they had founded and the colonial group they had formed in the Chamber of Deputies. Both agencies had influence and were indicative of the new spirit in metropolitan France.

Following the methods already evolved by the geographical societies in arousing interest in overseas expansion,[8] the colonial societies became ardent propaganda agencies devoted to the colonial cause; they expressed their enthusiasm by means of the many exploratory missions they sent to the French possessions, by the various publications they disseminated, and by the public lectures they sponsored. Chief among these societies was the Comité de l'Afrique française, which proudly listed among its members such celebrities as Paul Leroy-Beaulieu, Eugène Etienne, and later, Generals Gallieni and Lyautey. In 1894 the second most important society, the Union coloniale française, was founded by a group of financiers, merchants, and traders desirous of developing the colonies economically, Indochina in particular.[9]

Although the greatest efforts were made by these two organizations, others soon arose, so that by 1905 there were thirty-five in existence.[10] If the total number of members belonging to them was small in comparison with that of similar groups in other countries.[11] their influence was nevertheless apparent. Moreover, their endeavors were loosely combined with those of the colonial group in parliament.

Until the last decade of the nineteenth century anticolonialism had found its principal source in the French parliament. From the first days of the Third Republic un-

til the fall of Jules Ferry in 1885, numerous representatives
had reacted against all aspects of colonial policy. About
1890, however, the political atmosphere cleared to such an
extent that Eugène Etienne,[12] deputy from Oran and political heir of Ferry's colonial ideas, could establish a colonial group in the Chamber of Deputies in 1892. Number-
ing ninety-one members at the beginning, it obtained its
strength from the centrist parties, although members ad-
hered to it as a result of personal or local interests more
than as a result of party interests.[13] As in the French colonial societies, most of its members were former colonial
administrators, former military personnel, deputies representing coastal regions, and persons for whom imperialism
had become a national cause.

The chief purpose of the group was to control colonial
affairs in the Chamber of Deputies. Unfortunately, its influence and importance cannot be accurately assessed. Not
a regular parliamentary agency, the group kept no permanent records of its meetings, and little information about it
is available from other sources.[14] However, some idea of
the nature of its interests can be ascertained, for its members included a number of the theorists who, through pen
and speech, launched the attack upon traditional French colonial doctrine.

In this particular environment, created in the years 1889
and 1890 and lasting about two decades, a new concern
over colonial theory arose. While the problems which inspired this concern were many and the suggestions numerous as well, the issue around which the debate over theory

was largely centered was the advisability of the doctrine of assimilation as a basis for native policy.

Assimilation can be considered the traditional colonial doctrine of France. Although variously interpreted, in essence it meant that the colony was to become an integral, if noncontiguous, part of the mother country, with its society and population made over—to whatever extent possible—in her image. As one French critic of the idea wrote: "In France we confuse assimilation and uniformity. We are still with the old Platonic idea of universals. We want to model everyone in our own image, as if it had attained an absolute perfection, and as if all Frenchmen were alike." [15]

The simplicity, symmetry, and intrinsic appeal of the theory had long seduced those French minds which were concerned with colonial problems. Not only did assimilation appeal to the French love of order, belief in man's equality, and ever-present desire to spread French culture; it also appeared to provide for a uniform colonial administration.

Assimilation, by giving the colonies institutions analogous to those of metropolitan France, little by little removes the distances which separate the diverse parts of French territory and finally realizes their intimate union through the application of common legislation.[16]

The expression *France d'Outre-Mer* conveyed this thought.

At the end of the nineteenth century and more particularly in the first decade of the twentieth century, assimilation was analyzed and widely rejected. Condemned as rigid, unscientific, and harmful, assimilation was considered by most theorists no longer of any value to France's new and highly diversified colonial empire. Arguing in favor of a more realistic and flexible native policy, the new generation of colonial thinkers was desirous of gaining native cooperation and willing to respect native institutions. "Association" was the word most often employed to express the method they desired, and the policy of association was offered as the antidote to assimilation.

Around these words and the concepts which they represented, a debate over colonial theory and practice developed. Among its chief protagonists were colonial figures who had served in Indochina or who regarded that colonial region with considerable favor.[17] But almost all theorists, practiced in colonial administration or not, engaged in the discussion, for they saw the urgent need for a sound native policy if the new colonial empire was to be of value to France.

From 1890, when assimilation was last given wide sanction at the National Colonial Congress, until 1914, when all colonial problems paled before the terrible light of the First World War, colonial theory was given new consideration in metropolitan France.

Chapter 2

ORIGINS AND GROWTH OF THE
FRENCH DOCTRINE OF ASSIMILATION

IN large measure the history of French colonial theory, particularly in the nineteenth century, might be written as a history of the doctrine of assimilation. Because the concept of assimilation appeared attractive to the French, it found expression as a governing principle, if not a practice, during most periods of French colonial history. Yet the idea of assimilation itself was not exclusively French; its roots can be traced back into the far reaches of European civilization.[1]

Although the assimilative impulse is to be found at some time among most of the conquering peoples of the West, assimilation became conspicuous as a policy, in fact if not in name, during the days of the Roman Empire. At an early date Roman expansion led to Latinization of barbarian regions, as was particularly evident in Caesar's times. Cisalpine Gaul, for instance, in 49 B.C., enjoyed as a whole political equality with Rome. And in that same year Gades, in Spain, became the first community outside of Italy not founded by the Romans to gain the privileges of the Italian *municipia*. The famous *Constitutio Antoniana*, issued in the year

212 A.D. by the Emperor Caracalla, might also be considered to exemplify the idea of colonial assimilation. Regardless of the Emperor's motives for issuing the decree, it led to the legal absorption of vast numbers of peoples into the already extensive empire. No doubt the philosophic counterpart of decrees such as this one was the Stoic idea of the brotherhood of man in a world pervaded by reason, an idea which also enhanced the universal appeal of the imperial concept and thus helped create a feeling of solidarity among the many peoples owing allegiance to Rome.[2]

With the decay of the Roman Empire and the growth of Christianity, this Stoic thought was soon overshadowed by a religious one which bore a similar ecumenical message. The early Christians in preaching the equality of man in the sight of God soon developed the proselytizing spirit inherent in Christian teachings and converted much of the Western world to their religion. Again, at the end of the fifteenth century and the beginning of the sixteenth, this spirit was rekindled with the exploration of newly discovered, non-Christian regions of the world. Fulfilling Pope Alexander VI's desire to encourage the propagation of the faith, Spanish, Portuguese, and French missionaries, among others, carried the Christian message to the lands newly submitted to the control of their respective countries.

Assimilation now implied equality on a spiritual level as it had previously on a legal and philosophic one. Thus long before the French embodied assimilation in colonial theory, its practice had been apparent in diverse forms.

Origins of French Assimilation

In France the first definite indication of the assimilative
spirit was evidenced during the days of Richelieu. The
royal edicts of 1635 and 1642 stated that the natives, once
converted to Catholicism, were to be considered "citizens
and natural Frenchmen." [3] The Charter of the *Compagnie
des cents associés* also affirmed that Indians under its jurisdiction were to be led to the Catholic Faith and treated
thereafter as Frenchmen.[4] But in spite of these early endeavors, which were chiefly of a religious nature, assimilation, as a clearly enunciated principle of French colonial
policy, only became important during the decade of the
French Revolution. In fact it is the contention of some
writers that the Revolution saw the true birth of assimilation; or, as one writer put it, the idea of religious conver-
sion evident during the *ancien régime* was now translated
into political assimilation.[5]

At the beginning of the revolutionary period a policy
somewhat in variance with the political tenets of assimilation was pursued, undoubtedly out of necessity.[6] The re-
bellious spirit prevalent in the colonies at the time, the
growing bitterness among planter, merchant, and mulatto
over proposed regimes for the colonies, indicated that the
committee on colonies, appointed by the Constituent Assembly, would have to follow a middle road and thus avoid
excesses such as that of outright assimilation.[7] The solution
to this perplexing colonial problem was suggested by

Barnave, deputy from Dauphiné, in his speech of March 8, 1790. His suggestions became the basis of the moderate decree passed that same day by which the Assembly approved the existence of colonial assemblies and expressed its intention that no law on the status of nonfree persons be adopted unless first proposed by these assemblies.[8] Designed to conciliate the planters, the decree checked the ambitions of those persons desiring the abolition of slavery and a change in colonial regime. Later, a decree of September 24, 1791, permitted the colonies to initiate legislation which was then to be presented to the French legislative body. Subsequent encroachments upon the letter of this decree led to the dispatch of civil commissioners to the colonies in 1792, the sole result being that colonial administration was again left in a confused state.[9]

With the Constitution of the Year III, French colonial policy entered a new phase. François Antoine Boissy d'Anglas, a deputy keenly interested in constitutional matters and also in favor of a generous colonial policy, declared: "Attach the colonies to us by ties of common interest . . . so that they will be part of our indivisible republic and so that they will be protected and ruled by the same laws and the same government."[10] Heeding these words, the framers of the constitution affirmed in Article VI of that document: "The colonies are an integral part of the Republic and are subject to the same constitutional law."[11] Here was stated in succinct and clear form the idea of assimilation. Yet in so expressing themselves the French of 1795 were only fol-

lowing certain philosophic tendencies which had already
become an active part of French intellectual life: belief in
the power of reason and belief in the concept of universal
man.

That the philosophic origins of French assimilation
should be found in the Age of Reason is quite understandable. The rapid strides made in the physical sciences had
soon been imitated by the more humane or social sciences
which readily adopted scientific theories to their own uses
and thus provided fertile soil in which assimilation could
take root. Stimulated by the Newtonian concept of a
mechanistic universe and by Cartesian methods, given to
expressing the belief that "common sense is the one thing
most widely shared in the world," the philosophers of the
period began to think somewhat as mathematicians.[12] Led
to conclude that reason is universally persuasive and universally valued, they tended to base their theories on abstractions.

The genealogy of such ideas and their relation to assimilation are not difficult to trace. Thomas Hobbes sought to
erect a system of universal knowledge which would explain human activity in a manner similar to the explanation
of scientific phenomena by mathematical and physical systems. Then John Locke followed with his emphasis on em-
piricism and his own development of Hobbes's sensational-
ism. The celebrated idea of the mind being a *tabula rasa*
upon which knowledge and thoughts were inscribed by
sensation and experience was soon widely spread. It affected, among others, Claude Adrien Helvétius, a philos-

opher who may be named the intellectual father of the
French concept of assimilation.

Helvétius held to the sensationalist philosophy of Locke;
he felt that the mind was a creation of outside influences.
"Education makes us what we are," he affirmed; [13] mental
inequalities are the results of differences in education.[14]
Education, consequently, was of paramount importance to
Helvétius as a possible means of correcting discrepancies
between classes and other social groups. In these general
ideas can be discerned two important elements underlying
the doctrine of assimilation: the idea of basic human equality and the value of education as a corrective to environ-
mental differences.

Other philosophers added to this incipient body of
thought. The Encyclopedist D'Alembert placed great stress
on the need for universal enlightenment. Rousseau's belief
in the happy state of primitive nature and the ill effects of
society was so interpreted by the time of the Revolution
that many persons felt a type of lay morality, a brotherhood of man, could be assured once the causes of misery
and corruption were removed.[15] Condorcet also contributed to the belief in the betterment of mankind by em-
phasizing the progressive perfectibility of man. Add to this
notion his famous expression that "a good law is good for
all men," and the general ideas upon which French colonial
policy was to be based are clearly affirmed. Reason is the
virtue of the world; man is universally equal; law is everywhere applicable; societies are subject to rational alteration.

All of these ideas are found among the thoughts of the

revolutionaries, who often reflected the spirit of the age from which their own was emerging. The Abbé Siéyès captured the moment with his statement: "Two men, both being men, have, in equal degree, all the rights which derive from human nature." [16] And no better translation of such a thought into legislation is to be found than the Declaration of the Rights of Man and of the Citizen which emphatically states that "Men are born and live free and equal in rights." With its ecumenical and bellicose spirit, the Revolution developed into a secular crusade supposedly seeking to unfetter man from moribund but caste-ridden traditions. As in Europe, the principle of equality was broadcast in the French colonies which were now to be constitutional and administrative parts of continental France. Such an intention was embodied in the law of 12 Nivôse, Year VI, which regulated colonial organization and administration and which divided the colonies into departments like those already existing in metropolitan France.

Thus nourished by the Republic as a symbol of equality, the idea of assimilation never ceased henceforth to play an important role in colonial policy and doctrine. The idea, greatly stimulated by the republican egalitarian spirit, occupied a dominant position in colonial thought during the republican regimes which were yet to follow. A brief survey of subsequent colonial legislative history will show that after each period during which assimilation was deemphasized or apparently rejected, it was reasserted with renewed vigor.[17]

*Assimilation in Nineteenth-Century French
Colonial Legislation*

The successful growth of the idea of assimilation during
the Revolution was soon stunted with the advent of Napoleon as ruler of France. Although interested in colonial
matters, Napoleon remained sceptical about assimilation.
At first glance this attitude would seem curious, particularly in face of his own continental imperial policy which
resulted in the *Grand Empire*, parts of which were virtually
assimilated to France and subjected to the Napoleonic
Code. Actually, however, Napoleon's colonial policy was
the result of practical concerns, not doctrinal ones. Napoleon thought that in granting the colonies the same laws
as those of France, the colonists and natives would soon be
able to gain control of local governmental machinery and
would inevitably upset the economic regime of the remaining colonies, a regime dependent in his eyes on cheap
slave labor. Assimilation was therefore rejected, as was
obvious in the Constitution of 22 Frimaire, Year VIII,
which stated that the colonies would henceforth be regulated by separate laws.

The Charter of 1814 and that of 1830 scarcely changed
the underlying premises of the Napoleonic program, the
few colonies remaining under French control being governed generally by royal ordinances and separate laws. A
certain degree of autonomy in local matters was granted
to the governors and the colonial councils of the four large

colonies: Guadelóupe, Martinique, Réunion, and the Ile de Bourbon. Nevertheless, the spirit of assimilation was still alive during this period. For instance, Charles X's minister Hyde de Neuville remarked: "Aren't the colonies French? Are they not part of this large family?" To which questions he then answered: "The colonies are France." [18] And during the July Monarchy, on April 24, 1833, a law was passed according the enjoyment of all civil and political rights to all free persons in the colonies.

Again in 1848 the policy of assimilation was embraced.[19] Renan observed of the French Revolution of 1848 and its effects:

We wish to establish everywhere the government which is suitable to us and to which we have a right. We believe we are doing something marvelous by establishing a constitutional regime among the savages of Oceania, and soon we will send diplomatic notes to the Grand Turk requesting him to convoke his parliament.[20]

This remark was not malapropos, for the new government vigorously translated the traditional French republican ideas into legislation for the overseas regions. Encouraged in this direction by Victor Schoelcher, Undersecretary of State for Marine and Colonies, the government emancipated the slaves in the colonies by the decree of April 27. Then the Constitution of November 4 stated that the colonies were to be an integral part of French territory. To effect this policy, representatives from all the colonies were to be elected to the French Parliament, while Algeria was to be divided into three departments and subdivided into *arrondissements*, in administrative imitation of continental France. But such efforts—the essence of assimilation—were largely destroyed with the change of regime in France.

Nevertheless, the assimilative idea did not completely disappear during the reign of Napoleon III, a period which might well be considered a series of contradictions in colonial policy. The Constitution of January 14, 1852, a return to Bonapartism, declared anew a separate administration for the colonies. However, the *Senatus-Consulte* of 1854 and that of 1866 which modified it, both applying to Martinique, Guadeloupe, and Réunion, leaned toward assimilation. Important functions, such as local administration, the police, religion, the press, and even credit institutions, fell under the direct jurisdiction of the mother country. This same tendency was more subtly evident in Napoleon III's great colonial project for reform in Algeria.

In 1863 the Emperor wrote his famous letter to Governor-General Pelissier, expressing to the governor his interest in the idea of an "Arab Kingdom," one which would associate the French and the Arabs in such a way to convince the latter that "we have not come to Algeria to oppress and exploit them, but to bring them the benefits of civilization." [21] With such an objective in mind, Napoleon might have created a sort of Algerian protectorate but no such program ever crystallized, the only result being a decrease of local powers and the further introduction of French customs. The reporter of the *Senatus-Consulte* of 1865 truly explained this colonial development when he declared: "That which we are pursuing is a patient and continuous work of assimilation." [22] In this way the colonial policy of the Empire vacillated.

Thus it is not surprising that, Phoenix-like, the idea of assimilation again rose from the ashes of the Second Empire. Indeed it was during the early years of the Third Republic that assimilation became the central doctrine of French colonial policy, whenever that policy was considered ideologically. In a rash of laws and decrees the idea seemed to be realized. The colonies which existed in 1848 were again given the right to send representatives to parliament. Everywhere the French penal code was to be applied; the commune was adopted as the basis of local overseas government. Two extraparliamentary commissions in 1879 and in 1882, charged with the task of studying the possibilities of change in colonial administration, favored assimilation. Moreover, the tariff law of 1892 assimilated economically many overseas areas to France.[23]

As for Algeria, the famous Crémieux Decree of 1870 allowed the naturalization of the Jewish population within Algeria. Shortly thereafter, in the next year, Algeria received the right to elect deputies and, in 1875, senators. The decrees of *rattachement*, issued in 1881 and attaching the Algerian services to the various metropolitan ministries, were, however, the core of this new policy of assimilation. In almost all administrative matters, save those applying to the still existing military territories, the right of decision was taken from the governor-general and transferred to Paris. A decade later colonial reformers investigating the

Algerian problem were to denounce these *rattachements*,[24] but in 1881 they indicated in large measure the strength of assimilation.

Finally, the long delayed decision to establish a ministry of colonies seems to afford another example of the favorable sentiment then prevalent toward assimilation. Assimilation in its administrative sense implied *rattachements*, such as those mentioned above. As the theory ran, the colonies had no more need for a special ministry than did any of the metropolitan departments. This opinion, it has been averred,[25] explains why a separate ministry of colonies was so late in being established in France.

In every way the colonial policy of assimilation seemed to meet with success in matters of administration, while, in many instances, its success was evident among the upper classes of the native populations who had become assimilated to French culture in one way or another.

An Explanation of the Triumph of Assimilation

Yet the large colonial empire that France was rapidly amassing hardly lent itself to assimilation by the mother country. The new overseas regions were not *colonies de peuplement*, and, moreover, France with her relatively static population and well-known *casanier* spirit did not witness considerable migration to these regions. If a policy of assimilation had been possible in Martinique or in Canada, such was hardly the case in the new regions under French control in the late nineteenth century.

Many colonial theorists recognized this fact and consequently opposed assimilation. As will be seen in subsequent
chapters, they even found new sources of assistance from
the social sciences, particularly psychology and sociology,
which toward the end of the century were warning about
the dangers arising from interference with the laws of social
evolution and with the development of foreign mentalities.
Yet, regardless of the given nature of the colonial empire
and of new scientific theories, France, like King Canute,
seemed to howl at the rising tide of opposition and to continue to vaunt assimilation as a tenable colonial doctrine.

The reasons for this attitude are not difficult to find.
Certain factors are obvious. Chief among these is the French
penchant for administrative centralization. Already an active force during the *ancien régime*, as Tocqueville has
admirably shown, centralization increased with the Great
Revolution when it seemed politically desirable as a means
by which to stave off the reactionary forces of provincial-
ism.[26] Subsequently it has been a characteristic constant in
French administrative history. M. Pierre Lyautey went so
far as to write in his *L'Empire colonial français:* "There is
a dormant tendency toward centralization existing in every
Frenchman." [27] This tendency provides a partial explanation for the administrative assimilation that had taken place
overseas, particularly in Algeria.

In addition, the fact that French national interest was
initially directed ever so much more toward domestic problems and toward continental entanglements than toward
colonial ventures meant that the growing colonial empire

did not receive the attention it merited. New problems arising were either settled according to older, even outdated techniques or were momentarily ignored. In such an environment an interest in colonial doctrine and policy was slow in developing, and assimilation continued to survive. In fact it was even nourished by some of the representatives of the overseas regions themselves. As late as 1905, for instance, when assimilation was seriously attacked, M. Gerville-Réache, deputy from Martinique, continued to affirm that it was the best policy for France; he suggested that France and her colonies should form a single nation.[28] However, the weight of centralization or of France's domestic and continental interests was constantly felt and its effects can be measured in 1795, 1848, or even 1852.

What makes the period of the Third Republic so interesting in the matter of colonial doctrine is the force of some new but double-edged ideas derived from scientific thought and the then popular concepts of nationality which, on one side, were used to refute the idea of assimilation, while, on the other, lent new life to the doctrine. The opponents of assimilation, as will be discussed later, denounced the doctrine because it was abstract and unable to accommodate itself to the expressed scientific thought that races and peoples must and do evolve in their own particular national and cultural environments and hence have their own particular national characteristics. Yet this very trend of thought also seemed to lead to the conclusion that assimilation was a natural part of French intellectual life and as French a doctrine as wine is a drink.

In the later part of the nineteenth century the subject of *Volkspsychologie* seized the imagination. Today one is not likely to make sweeping generalizations about the nature and characteristics of any nation or people, but the pioneers of the nineteenth century entered this province with spirits high. National psychology had its vogue, and one coincidental with Social Darwinism.

The organic concept of society, which owed much of its popularity to the labors of Herbert Spencer, was greatly emphasized in France at the end of the century and became accepted as an easy means for analyzing a multitude of problems pertaining to society and politics. Of chief interest was the idea that a society had an organic structure similar to that of a human being. The cells of the social organism were the individuals living within it; national traits were hereditary so that the present could only be understood through the past and could not be divorced from it.

The conclusion drawn from this assumption was that nations like individuals have characteristics which cannot be changed overnight and which are only really understood when the growth of the organism itself is analyzed. According to Alfred Fouillée, a philosopher-sociologist of great reputation:

The nation is an organism endowed with a kind of collective consciousness, although not concentrated in an ego; I therefore take everything that maintains in a nation continuity of character, mind, habits, and aptitudes—in a word, a national consciousness and a national will—as a form of organic heredity persisting from age to age.[29]

Each nation then was blessed with a personality of its own, and, according to her analysts, France had one that could scarcely be called dull. While historians of the calibre of Michelet and Hanotaux appraised and lauded those qualities which put France above her neighbors, the one serious attempt to analyze the French national personality was delightfully made by Fouillée in *Psychologie du peuple français*. The part of the work which is of value here is entitled *Psychologie de l'esprit français* and begins with the interesting challenge: "Let's try to discover the true physiognomy of the French spirit." [30]

Analyzing French sensitivity, Fouillée remarked first that the French are an excitable people, the physiological fact for this seeming to be "a hereditary excess of tension in the nerve and sensory centers." [31] But this sensitivity manifests itself in a centrifugal or expansive direction. For the French have a highly developed social instinct which makes them feel the need to be in harmony with other people.

Thus we are often naive enough to believe that that which makes us happy will make everyone happy, that all of humanity must think and feel as France does. Hence our proselytism, the contagious character of our national spirit which often ends by alluring other nations despite the indifference of some and the cautious defiance of others.[32]

Along with this expansive spirit, the French character is endowed with an exceptionally active intelligence, an ability to seize upon an idea without difficulty. This rapid perception results in the love of clarity and a tendency toward simplification. The Frenchman, therefore, does not generally have a strong imagination but rather is possessed of a "love for reasoning." And in his choice of ideas, those which have a social or humane character "will be particularly in harmony with the French spirit." [33]

From Fouillée's analysis emerges the picture of the Frenchman as a highly rational being endowed with a logical mind, a tendency to simplify, and a desire to deal in universal equations. But this refinement of mind did not result from spontaneous generation. The effects of social evolution were not to be denied, insisted many French critics. Here Fouillée found himself in accord with Michelet, who measured the importance of the Latin and Christian inheritance on French development. "France has continued the work of Rome and the Christian Church. Fraternal equality, formerly postponed until the hereafter, has been taught to the world by France as the law of the here-and-now." [34] Wrote Fouillée in a similar tone:

The evolution of the French spirit has passed from Roman to Christian universality, and from that to a purely human universality; the time has not yet come to break through the concentric circles. By separating ourselves violently from our origins, we would be separating ourselves from the very principles of our spiritual life. [35]

Supposedly, it was this Latin-Christian tradition which originally gave to France her universal outlook and her emphasis on equality. Certain elements of Stoic philosophy incorporated into Roman thought and Roman Law provided the basis for universal law while the Christian emphasis on the equality of man before God provided the basis for secular equality. Here are found the roots of the French love of order, the desire to codify all laws natural and human in a logical fashion,[36] and the tendency to express everything in universal terms.

If the ideas concerning the essential nature of the French character are viewed in connection with the thought of the Enlightenment, then the contemporary observer can understand why the French mind has produced the formal gardens of Versailles. He can also understand why the philosopher Etienne Gilson wrote the epigram: "Notre particularité, c'est notre universalité."

With this intellectual background projected before their eyes, many French imperialists saw the idea of colonial assimilation as part of France's Latin nature. Particularly noted by authors of works dealing with colonial matters was the influence of the Roman heritage. Many would agree with Pierre Lyautey, who wrote in 1931 that France was "born of Rome whose law gave particular attention to the status of foreigners and barbarians." [37] Earlier, Arthur Girault, Professor of Law at the University of Poitiers and author of a highly successful and long-lived text on colonial legislation, affirmed that assimilation was the policy of "nations of the Latin race, faithful heirs of the Roman spirit of assimilation." [38] Almost repeating Girault's words, Arnaud and Méray, in their *Les Colonies françaises: organisation administrative, judiciaire, politique et financière*, contended that assimilation "has been the preference of peoples of Latin origins, thus imitating the methods of Roman civilization." [39] The validity of such statements was questioned, it is true,[40] but the popularity of the Roman idea as thus conceived did not wane.

Still another popular idea, one closely allied with the analysis of French nature described above, exercised its influence on French colonial theory: the *mission civilisatrice*. Certainly the French were not alone in expressing such a thought, as any glance at the colonial history of the time will show,[41] but they emphasized it more than any other people.

Few persons who have enjoyed the delights of French civilization have failed to realize that the French, proud of their attainments in the intellectual realm, hold their proverbial *flambeau de civilisation* high so that all may see it. No less an observer than the novelist Henry James wrote to the *New York Tribune* in 1876:

Whether or not as a nation the French are more conceited than their neighbors is a question that may be left undecided; a very good case on this charge might be made out against every nation. But certainly France occasionally produces individuals who express the national conceit with a transcendent fatuity which is not elsewhere to be matched. A foreign resident in the country may speak upon this point with feeling; it makes him extremely uncomfortable. I don't know how it affects people who dislike French things to see their fantastic claims for their spiritual mission in the world, but it is extremely disagreable for those who like them. Such persons desire to enjoy in a tranquil and rational manner the various succulent fruits of French civilization but they have no fancy for being committed to perpetual genuflections and prostrations.[42]

The Frenchman Alfred Fouillée saw this matter in an entirely different light, however. He wrote:

A nation, like an individual, has its own instinct and genius. It has the more or less vague sense of its "mission" to humanity. If social science rejects every mystical interpretation of the common spirit animating a nation, it by no means rejects the reflected consciousness or spontaneous divination of it.[43]

While Fouillée saw republicanism, with its accompanying ideas of liberty and equality, as the most obvious objective for France, many other Frenchmen, particularly the defenders of France's new colonial empire, spoke of France's civilizing mission toward less developed peoples. No one put the idea more succinctly than Charles Castre who wrote as late as 1922: "There lives in French hearts a spontaneous piety (in the nature of a spiritual instinct) for the civilizing mission to which France has ever dedicated herself." [44] Yet earlier writers had said much the same thing. In a book entitled *L'Energie française* Gabriel Hanotaux wrote:

Races are great and powerful because of the importance and prospects of the tasks which have been assigned them.

Let me be clearly understood: this is not only a matter of a vast number of conquests; it is not even a matter of the increase of public and private wealth. It is a question of extending overseas to regions only yesterday barbarian the principles of a civilization of which one of the oldest nations of the world has the right to be proud. It is a question of creating near us and far away from us so many new Frances; it is a question of protecting our language, our customs, our ideals, the French and Latin glory, in face of furious competition from other races, all marching along the same routes.[45]

And finally, listen to A. Demangeon in his essay *La Politique coloniale*, written shortly after World War I and critical of assimilation: "Nearly an instinctive movement of national temperament, this tendency [to fraternize] became an idea: in effect, it became the doctrine of France, champion of equality and of fraternity toward colonial peoples." [46]

The form of cultural imperialism which was bound to result from such questionable moralizing contained the notion of the right of a "superior" society to dominate and instruct a "lesser" one. Clearly put, the conquered were to absorb the customs and institutions of the conquerors; it was the "white man's burden" translated into the French by the word "assimilation." Partly because such thoughts were seductive to the French, and partly because they helped allay fears about the expense and possible foolhardiness of overseas ventures, ideas like "duty" and "civilizing mission" were broadcast by the imperialists of the late nineteenth century, anxious as they were to justify their stand to a nation traditionally anti-colonial.

One can only hazard a guess as to what effect the elevation of the republican ideals of this period to secular dogma —the result of radicalism and neo-Jacobinism, of the *nation doctrinaire*, as Thibaudet described it— [47] had on the acceptance of current clichés concerning colonial doctrine. With the famous struggle leading to the laic laws of 1881, republican ideals were vaunted in face of clerical opposition, and these ideals had their tap roots in revolutionary ideology, in the famous triad of liberty, equality, and fraternity. The vocabulary relating to the doctrine of assimilation and that relating to these republican ideals were the same. Moreover, the victory of republicanism came at the beginning of the new colonial era. Thus French ears attuned to republican phraseology also found familiar the phraseology in which the expansion of France overseas was justified. Furthermore, it has been said that assimilation was particularly pushed during the two periods in which the republicans were in power, in 1871 and after 1879.[48]

Everything considered, it can scarcely be surprising that assimilation should have become the outstanding French colonial doctrine and, moreover, often considered all but part of the natural order of things. Even though the vast majority of Frenchmen never reflected on colonial theory, those who did established a line of thought which was consistent with the Revolutionary philosophy and its subsequent development. Indeed, what could seem more logical to so many of the French than a general application of the principles found in the Declaration of the Rights of Man and of the Citizen?

Thus by the beginning of the last decade of the nineteenth century the traditional doctrine of assimilation still seemed healthily exuberant. The National Colonial Congress of 1889–90 was the moment of its apparent success. Senator Issac, who was president of this assemblage, proposed to the Congress the resolution: "That the efforts of colonization in all countries under French authority be directed in the sense of the propagation among the natives of the national language, the mores and the processes of work of the *métropole*." [49] After slight modification the resolution was accepted with almost no opposition.[50] Never had assimilation seemed to be more loudly affirmed. According to the historian of French colonial policy, Stephen Roberts: "Liberty, equality and fraternity were in the air, all constructed on the best orthodox lines of the *Code Napoléon* and eighteenth century reason; and France saw Papeete and Dakar and Insulah only as the distant suburbs of Paris." [51]

Yet this moment of assimilation's apparently complete triumph marked the end of one period in the history of French colonial theory and the beginning of another. With the decade of 1890 doctrinal matters assumed hitherto unknown importance. The empire was established and accepted. The new climate of opinion enabled theorists to give up their defensive position and to reflect more thoroughly on the problems of colonial administration. As a result of observation, study and the influence of the new social sciences, the theorists who expressed their ideas about native policy in the period following 1890 became, almost to a man, strongly opposed to the principle of assimilation.

Chapter 3

IDEAS FROM ABROAD

THE rapid growth of imperialism in the last decades of the nineteenth century could not help but arouse an interest in comparative colonial studies.[1] France witnessed the publication of a number of books devoted to the colonial practices of the European powers, several of which were written by theorists who turned their attention to those colonial nations whose methods and experience appeared valuable. The vastness and newness of the second French colonial empire were awesome, while memories of the first colonial empire usually served for little except to remind the imperialists that a similar fate should not await the newly acquired overseas regions. French colonial experience of a contemporary nature, particularly in tropical regions already populated, was lacking. Largely as a result, an intense if limited interest in studies of comparative colonization developed. It was one which was to have a definite influence on the French colonial theory of the period.

The need for this effort was perhaps first clearly signaled by Paul Leroy-Beaulieu in his *De la colonisation chez les peuples modernes*. This imposing book, one of the classic studies of modern colonization, was first published in 1874

and had an influence which did not cease to grow with subsequent editions.[2] The careful survey of various contemporary colonial systems and the interesting evaluation of
them more than succeeded in fulfilling the author's intention to seek among colonial powers "the body of precepts
which comprised the art of colonization." [3] Indeed, the results of Leroy-Beaulieu's efforts seemed to prepare the way
and to set the pace for subsequent studies which, through
an analysis of foreign colonial practices, helped France
answer her more urgent questions of colonial policy.

In particular, what most French imperialists interested in
the matter sought from their rivals was a solution to the
essential problem of governing native populations in such a
way as to make the colonies prosper. The problem was
rather new to them; in fact, their sole recent experience of
long duration was in Algeria where a policy of assimilation
had been attempted. But the majority of contemporary
theorists firmly rejected this practice, looking upon its
results with strong disfavor. Their opinion was bitterly
summed up by one writer in a single sentence: "With our
pretended humanitarian systems, we need 60,000 soldiers
to maintain peace in Algeria." [4] In spite of the admirable
efforts of people like Paul Cambon in Tunisia and Paul
Bert in Indochina, the French government was still accused
of lacking a good colonial policy and of following instead an administrative policy cloaked in the name of assimilation.[5]

The retreat from a policy of assimilation appeared to
grow in direct proportion to the French admiration for
foreign colonial methods and techniques. The variety of

studies was interesting. Colonial authorities, turned authors, drew dogmatic conclusions from their studies; several professors published new texts on various types of colonialism, while aspiring university candidates found a rich, new source for individual research.[6] Yet in most cases the selection of models and masters to be followed was limited. Italy and Spain received no real attention. Germany was given scant treatment, and one author dismissed that nation's colonial policy in the following fashion: "There is no need to speak of Germany which, from its beginnings in colonial affairs to the present, has neither developed in theory nor realized in practice any colonial doctrine whatsoever." [7] The writers who were interested in American imperialism were either critical or condescending. Some simply restricted their analyses to the question of the Monroe Doctrine and its Roosevelt Corollary as aspects of international law.[8] But the new French and American spheres of activity were hardly contiguous, and distance still separated the nations geographically and mentally.

Nevertheless the French, as "newcomers to colonialism," [9] were thought able to profit from the efforts of two peoples who, after many painful errors, had finally arrived at what appeared to be a sound colonial policy. These were the Dutch and the British.

Dutch Colonial Methods as Viewed by the French

In the French books and articles dedicated to Dutch administration in the East Indies, there was to be found a strong sentiment in favor of Dutch colonial policies. The

thing which struck the French imagination was the manner
in which this veritable empire, three times the size of
France and with a population of some 34,000,000, was effectively and profitably governed by a small group of European bureaucrats.

The primary reason given for Dutch success was the
elaboration of a native policy which had as its basis the
maintenance of native institutions.[10] Instead of abolishing
the older native administration, it was said, the Dutch gave
the illusion of power to local princes and to the native
hierarchy who served as intermediaries for the Dutch resident officials.[11] Such a relationship was thought to be most
advantageous as it catered to the "extraordinary love of
Orientals for public functions and social distinctions." [12]

This Dutch policy, moreover, appeared to be unique.[13]
One author lauded the fact that the princes and important
native dignitaries continued to exercise, almost without
modification, their ancient functions, while the Dutch administration penetrated this older feudal administration
from above, never touching its lower levels.[14] All that the
Dutch required from the native princes was acknowledge-
ment that the exercise of their privileges henceforth was
dependent upon the Dutch. This was the statement of
Joseph Chailley-Bert, an outstanding colonial theorist of
his time.[15] To the question of what led the Dutch to maintain the illusion of native power, Chailley-Bert replied that
it was the "Dutch repugnance for innovation and systemiza-
tion"; it was also their respect for experience and tradition.
Above all it was a "certain bonhomie resulting from in-

telligence and indulgence which has enabled them to understand the native mentality" and to respect native life, even
its weaknesses.[16]

Yet, despite this praise for Dutch colonial policy in the
Far East, the French were not blind to the fact that the
Dutch themselves had gone through a period of errors of
a most grave nature. In France, as elsewhere, the Culture
System fostered by General Van den Bosch, who tried to
regain Dutch prosperity in the East Indies after the
Napoleonic period and the English occupation of the region, was considered regrettable.[17] The type of forced labor
this system inevitably entailed was condemned, and the
demoralization and unrest of the native populations had
been all too apparent to French as well as to Dutch eyes.[18]
Toward the middle of the century economic liberalism was
encouraged in the Dutch East Indies and the Culture System
was abolished. Thereafter Dutch administration seemed
more lenient and considerate. In the opinion of Chailley-
Bert the "little Javanese" was now protected by the local
administration of the Dutch rather than exploited by it.
"This was more than a policy," he concluded; "It was a
movement of the heart." [19]

Such a growing respect for native customs and institutions won the favor of French writers who felt that the
prosperity and increasing population of the Dutch East
Indies were the direct results of the sound colonial policy
practiced there. A method based on the thorough study of
colonial problems and their solution according to both native and European interests supposedly pushed the Dutch

far ahead in the art of colonization.[20] This method, remarked Edgard Denancy in his book, *Philosophie de la
colonisation*, was the best ever utilized by a European
power.[21] According to him, its essence was found in the
carefully studied development of each colony, as if the
colony were a well-cared-for farm.[22]

Apparent to the French was the fact that the Dutch
sought to reconcile native interests with European ones in
a manner quite unlike that characteristic of assimilation.[23]
This endeavor was sometimes called a "policy of association," [24] whereby the native was made an associate of the
European in developing the colonial region. Even though
the Dutch colonies were not autonomous and the king's
representatives wielded quasi-omnipotent powers, the Dutch
system was still admired because its goal was considered a
political and commercial one, divorced from ideas of
proselytism.[25] These views were a clear rebuttal of traditional French colonial doctrine as well as of the centralization and assimilation it entailed. A similar judgment, albeit
more fully expressed, was made of British colonial efforts.

The Influence of English Ideas and Ideals on French Colonial Theory

Toward the end of the nineteenth century many articu-
late Frenchmen sang praise of the English and their institutions and even sought to convince their compatriots of
the value of emulating the activities of their *outre-manche*
neighbors. This Anglomania was not new, as witness the

eighteenth century and, indeed, most of the nineteenth century, when many French eyes regarded England with favor. Now, however, the industrial and financial might of Great Britain stood out vividly, metaphorically illuminated by a sun which never set on British soil. The apparent material success of their insular neighbors inspired Frenchmen to admiration, or to a respect tempered by fear for a people who, it was declared, had boundless expansive qualities and a seeming propensity to dominate the world. Many French writers were concerned about this increasing Anglo-Saxon domination and were interested in following Taine's objective put forth in his *Histoire de la littérature anglaise,* which was "to arrive at a definition of the English temperament." [26] Hence they devoted themselves to analyzing the Englishman, or more broadly, the "Anglo-Saxon."

What accounted for Anglo-Saxon "aggressiveness," "self-confidence," and "superiority" became questions of wide interest and the matter of many publications. In an age when anthropology and psychology were exciting contemporary minds, the way was clear for all sorts of speculation: critical study, pseudoscientific theory, and plain nonsense.

Out of this literature emerged a description of the factors which were thought to be responsible for the formation of the much admired Anglo-Saxon character. They were explained somewhat as follows. The unpleasant climate of the British Isles and the subsequent need to struggle for a sufficient material existence there nourished the growth of initiative and of foresight among the population. [27] Upbringing, beginning with the training of the nursery, taught the young Englishman the value of "self-help," the need for initiative,[28] and hardened him to the dangers of the outside world.[29] Boundless energy and the love of physical exertion endowed him with drive and, was, in part, the cause of his aggressiveness.[30] Education, although considered inferior to that of other countries, was designed to produce the "whole man," one whose general culture might be weak, but whose native curiosity was strong and whose self-confidence was firmly fixed.[31]

These qualities attributed to the Anglo-Saxon were the envy of most of the French authors who analyzed them and who felt that their own countrymen lacked anything comparable.[32] Such opinion was vigorously maintained by Edmond Démolins in *A quoi tient la supériorité des Anglo-Saxons?*, a book which marked the high water mark in the wave of praise for all things Anglo-Saxon and which merits a few words here.[33]

Démolins, an ardent disciple of Le Play, sought to analyze the reasons for Anglo-Saxon "superiority." Following the assertions of the other Anglophiles, he stated that it was the "particularistic formation" of the Anglo-Saxons which accounted for their remarkable strides.[34] Gradually freed from Norman and Celtic influences, which were "communistic" in that they subordinated the individual to society and the state,[35] the Anglo-Saxon racial element was responsible for the development of a unique type of individual, unfettered by state control and tenacious of his personal freedom. Above all, he was "particularistic," averse to the paternalism which characterized other European peoples, particularly the French. Rugged individualist, the Anglo-Saxon sought no easy sinecure from the state; never was he satisfied to be a minor bureaucrat. Rather, trained from youth to combat successfully in the struggle for existence, he depended solely on his own efforts, forged ahead, and, in a sense, carved the world with his own hands. What is here described is the typical character from Horatio Alger: the self-made man worthy of leadership. For Démolins insisted that the essential law of personal labor consisted in gaining one's bread by the sweat of one's brow.[36] This, in essence, he contended, accounted for Anglo-Saxon superiority over other peoples. There was only one conclusion to be drawn from such an analysis: France's "hereditary rival" should be emulated.[37]

Démolins's book was rather well received.[38] Many critics felt that it ably described the sad truth, while some were even thankful that it was a Frenchman and not an Englishman who had exposed what many had bitterly felt. As Jules Lemaître wrote in *Figaro*:

What stands out from this exposé, which is as convincing as it is lamentable, is the immense social, political, commercial, industrial, financial and moral superiority of the Anglo-Saxon race; also, it is our weakness, our misfortune and our worthlessness which stand out. For the superiority of our vaudevillists and of our cooks will not save us. And it could be that our artistic superiority itself has been but a useless luxury.[39]

While dissenting voices scoffed at the opinions held by the Anglophiles and ably refuted them,[40] the general atmosphere of admiration had an intoxicating effect on French colonial theorists.

This fact remains true in spite of the existing colonial

rivalry between the two nations: "Greater France" was now vying with "Greater Britain." [41] In such a competition experience was considered a primary asset, yet one which obviously could not be acquired overnight. Here was a problem which deeply concerned the French. It led them, in part, to turn their attention toward their imperialistic neighbor. Moreover, encouragement was probably supplied by the British imperialists themselves who were not loath to heap praise on their own system.[42] It took no imagination to see that the British Empire stood out as a forceful example. Britain had a long, uninterrupted colonial history which encompassed a vast variety of peoples and climates. Moreover, she had made fundamental mistakes, had profited from them, and now appeared to be stronger than ever as a colonial power. France, it thus seemed, could not pick a better model.

Even before Anglomania had reached a high pitch in France, colonial writers had expressed a desire to learn from their neighbors across the Channel. As early as 1885 Alfred Rambaud and Colonel Baille had translated J. B. Seeley's famous *Expansion of England* into French, for they felt that the study was "full of lessons from which the French must profit." [43] Chief among these lessons was the one that emphasized the immense value of a colonial empire.[44] While Seeley was fostering the imperialist cause in Great Britain by popularizing it, the timely translation of his book helped fix French attention on his country's imperialist policies.

The supposedly superior colonial methods employed by the British seemed to many French writers the natural out-

growth of the Anglo-Saxon genius.[45] This is not to say
that the French denied their own ability to help shoulder
the "white man's burden." While Rhodes and Kipling spoke
highly of the Anglo-Saxon as being conscious of his duty
to mankind, certain French writers also spoke of their own
like responsibilities. Whether as a mother country charged
with the task of ultimately creating "daughters of its race,
heiresses of its genius" [46] or as a strong nation needing to
give its support to weaker peoples,[47] France was also present and prepared.

Meanwhile, interest in so-called "imperial races" and
fascination with ancient Roman grandeur were becoming
popular. If one were to believe the novelists of both countries, the Roman inheritance was shared by both people.
Louis Bertrand's heroes were conscious that they were
"neo-Latins"; Somerset Maugham's Alec McKenzie took
pride in being a part of a "greater Rome." [48] But the French
imperialists, apparently less imbued with the Latin spirit
than their literary compatriots, were more inclined to be
on the side of the British novelists who placed chief emphasis on the importance of the Anglo-Saxon element in
the creation of a new imperial tradition.

Among the French there was a tendency to contrast
French and British policies; the French invariably came out
a poor second. Scored by their own countrymen, French
colonial administrators were accused of trying to transport
their civilization across the seas with the intention of be-
stowing it on colonial peoples who were then to become
français de couleur.[49] No such *mission civilisatrice* spurred

the British on to a latter-day crusade, the argument continued.[50] Guided only by utilitarian goals, the British sought
to solve the one essential problem, that of achieving colonial
prosperity.[51] Practical, aggressive, and profiting from vast
experience, this businesslike people knew how to make economic arrangements most profitable to itself. This theme is
often repeated, as a sampling from French writing on the
subject will indicate. Concerning the French and English
in India, one Frenchman wrote: "The Englishman hasn't
the false pretension to be loved; he wishes to be comforta-
ble and to 'make money.' His goal has been attained." [52]
In discussing the need for reform of French colonial administration, another wrote of the British and their Indian
Service: "A people for whom all problems take the form
of business affairs seems to us to have attained the ideal in
so far as this is possible." [53] And still another wrote: "The
English have colonies in order to do business; we have
them in order to give positions to our bureaucrats." [54] In
contrast to the French empire, as yet unprofitable, the
British Empire made a picture of prosperity and vigor. Impressed by this scene, many of the French colonial theorists
suggested that British methods be copied, or at least adapted
to French conditions.

The apparent variety of organization and administration
within the British Empire was the striking feature to French
eyes. Far from the universalistic concept of French doctrine, the British seemed to shun the idea of only one type
of organization because "their practical spirit has rapidly
led them to understand the sorrows it ultimately pro-

duces." [55] Therefore, they were never "so foolish as to believe that the same system was suitable for all these peoples." [56] Instead, their administration was decentralized and
generally based on the particular conditions of the region's
economic, social, and ethnic development.[57] In addition the
English were credited with utilizing existing administrative machinery and with allowing the natives to have a
hand in government. Thus averred one writer: "In order
to govern her colonies England utilizes the elements she
finds of the spot while France imports hers from home.
There is scarcely need to say that the first system is the
better." [58] Echoing this thought, but in somewhat caustic
terms, another Frenchman wrote:

The English allow their subjects to govern themselves because that is how they themselves are governed. . . . And we
French, we also follow a similar natural tendency when we
apply to Africans and Asiatics the wisely detailed mechanism
of an administration thanks to which a Frenchman in France
can't light his cigar without exposing himself to two or three
kinds of infraction of the law.[59]

The French also applauded another feature which they
considered part of the English colonial characteristics:
aloofness in place of fraternity with regard to the natives.
Eugène Aubin, a member of the French colony in Egypt
and a very interested observer of the British techniques
employed there, declared that the lack of a proselytizing
spirit resulted from the fact that the British considered
themselves "an imperial race, made for universal domination . . . and too disdainful to initiate inferior races in the
secrets of their superiority." [60]

Other opinions were less bitterly worded but indicated the same idea of an English "hands-off" policy. The French thought that rather than introduce European institutions to peoples unprepared for them, the English realized the first need of primitive societies was "a regime which develops their initiative, teaches them responsibility and favors their economic development." [61] The results of these practices were deemed favorable, for, as the Colonial Congress of 1905 was told, "the native holds the English in admiration for their justice, their aloofness and their impassibility." [62]

Views of the British in the Far East

If praise was often almost unreserved for the general features of British colonial policy, it was equally warmly expressed for the methods employed in England's Asiatic possessions which bore strong resemblance to the French territories in this region. This vast regional empire, of which India was truly the jewel, was hailed as a "marvelous spectacle." [63]

Imitation of it was heartily encouraged by a few stalwarts. Jules Harmand, one of the most important theorists of the time, remarked that the English themselves had borrowed from the experience of Dupleix in the eighteenth century; why could not the inverse be true in the nineteenth century? [64] A similar thought was expressed in the introduction to the translation of *British India* by Sir Richard Temple. Jean-L. de Lanessan, a governor-general of

Indochina, stated that "the French can herein learn how a colony is founded, administered and enriched for the greatest profit to the natives, the colonists and the mother country." [65] A few years later, two other books were published which were also studies of the British methods in this region and which had similar objectives. The one was *Colonisation de l'Indo-Chine; l'expérience anglaise,* by Joseph Chailley-Bert, and the other was a translation by Jules Harmand of Sir John B. Strachey's *India.* Both Chailley-Bert and Harmand wielded an important influence on the formation of contemporary colonial theory.

Joseph Chailley, or Chailley-Bert as he called himself after becoming the son-in-law of Paul Bert, had, according to one French writer, an enormous influence on French colonial thought, his works inspiring a generation of colonials.[66] That he himself was inspired by the work and ideas of his father-in-law, whom he served as personal assistant in Indochina in 1886, he has clearly acknowledged in the preface to *Colonisation de l'Indo-Chine; l'expérience anglaise.*[67] Although Bert died of dysentery after less than a year in Indochina, he had already outlined a policy of local administration which inspired his son-in-law and which was presented by him in the volume *Paul Bert au Tonkin,* published in 1887.

Chailley-Bert was an indomitable champion of French overseas expansion. He had traveled to the Far East to observe first-hand the colonial activities there; at home he assumed a position in the vanguard of his generation of imperialists. Not only was he a deputy for a time but also he

was an officer in several of the burgeoning colonial societies. His writings on colonial affairs are quite extensive, and
his name was well-known to Frenchmen fostering the imperialist cause. As a colonial theorist he contended that the
newly reconstituted French colonial empire suffered from
a lack of methods and men to execute them so that the development of the empire could be accomplished.[68] The
earlier French colonial experience was no longer of value
because it had been interrupted in its evolution. Hence the
guides necessary to lead the French through their current
colonial difficulties and to reeducate them in colonial matters had to be sought abroad. To the Dutch and the British
Chailley-Bert turned, but chiefly to the British. Nevertheless, he was cautious in this movement for he realized that
the profit to be derived from study of foreign colonial systems could be exaggerated. Still, he thought that France
could find two elements of value for herself in British colonization:

The first, an experience at the same time tried, uninterrupted,
and contemporary . . . and the second, a just defiance of im-
provisation and the appreciation, one hundred times confirmed,
that in the conduct of colonial affairs nothing can take the place
of experience or even of mere study.[69]

Chailley-Bert considered that this might be all the British
could teach the French but the understanding of just this
was not an easy task. What he set out to do in *Colonisation
de l'Indo-Chine* was to determine what the French could
learn of value from the British experience in Hong Kong
and Burma.

Although both regions were studied in detail, much the same general conclusions emerge for both. What Chailley-Bert praised was the British method of trying to adapt administrative machinery to the given colonial situation, of providing decentralized authority, of fostering economic liberalism and hence encouraging private capital within the context of a laissez-faire policy, and, last, of having able colonial officials. Here supposedly was the inverse of what was to be found in the French colonial experience of the day.

The underlying theme of this work might well have been: how to make a colony prosper. Student of Léon Say, the grandson of J. B. Say, Chailley-Bert leaned to the classical school of economics in a day when tariff walls were everywhere being hastily erected and when France had fostered a colonial system of economic protection. He believed that the French were stifling the growth of their colonies by pursuing only a course leading to immediate economic ends and by failing to wait until the colonies would prosper. Touching upon an idea he was later to elaborate, Chailley-Bert insisted that the prosperity of the colonies could not be obtained in the present but could only be obtained in the future, in perhaps thirty or forty years when the colony's economy had been stimulated sufficiently by the capitalists.[70] He was thus against the idea of immediate market value in the colonies, and, in fact, deemed the home manufacturers detrimental to the colonies, for all they sought was preferential treatment for their goods.[71] To Chailley-Bert the capitalists on the spot, the colonists themselves, could alone guarantee that the colony would be economically sound and advantageous to the mother country. To arrive at this state, the colonial regions would have to be able to import and export as they saw fit. Thanks to such a sensible economic policy, the colony's wealth would increase, its trade having been stimulated, and hence it would be economically self-sufficient and no longer a drain on the mother country's budget. This, insisted Chailley-Bert, was the type of policy the British were sagely pursuing in both Hong Kong and Burma.[72]

If the English economic policy was the chief attraction to Chailley-Bert, it was scarcely the sole one. He greatly admired the flexibility of the British colonial system as well.[73] Colonies within it were not rigidly categorized, and the colonists enjoyed an important role in colonial administration and policy. Even in Hong Kong, a crown colony, administrative centralization was tempered by local control under competent authorities.[74] Then again, the British were more timorous than the French, not insisting, as did the French, that their legal codes were good and applicable anywhere. The British felt that all legislation must "vary with the latitudes" and that each country should only receive those laws which are appropriate to its own needs.[75]

That the English in Burma had not yet succeeded in pacifying the country or even in establishing a good administration at the time Chailley-Bert's book appeared was an obvious fact. Yet this did not cause the author a moment's hesitation; he simply declared that the "mediocrity of the results proves nothing against the method."[76] Instead of pursuing a policy of expediency which might have given the appearance of initial success, the English had adopted a far more conscientious program. They were assuring the future by efforts carefully planned in the present; they were constructing on a solid and durable base. Thus, if to untrained eyes the French in the region of Tonkin seemed to be far more advanced than the English in Burma, Chailley-Bert answered that this was nothing but an illusion. The English would soon outstrip the French because their policy would assure the future welfare of the colony.[77]

From these observations Chailley-Bert concluded that the French should adapt the English methods to the conditions of Indochina.[78] The English experience enabled the French to follow certain rules which would be of value there.[79] These were as follows. First, it was necessary to study the ethnic composition of the peoples living on the peninsula. Second, French administrators should draft laws harmonious with the native legal system. Third, trained colonial personnel should be introduced in order to assure the careful application and interpretation of these laws. Fourth, the system of the protectorate should be restored so that native support could be gained and the security of the country thus guaranteed.[80] Fifth, public works and education should be improved. And last, wealthy colonists, capitalists, should be called forth, with monopolies and special economic privileges offered them.

On the whole, the ideas of Chailley-Bert ran parallel to those of Jules Harmand as the latter expressed them in his

preface to *India*. As a physician in the colonial service
Harmand had acquired invaluable experience serving with
François Garnier in the Delta region of Tonkin in 1873.
This experience was even further enriched when he was
Commissaire général of the region in 1883. The following
year, as consul-general for France at Calcutta, he became
greatly impressed with the English administration of the
subcontinent of India and thought that the French could
profit handsomely from the English experiences. With this
purpose in mind, he had the intention, upon his return to
France, of writing a book which would explain the virtues
of this colonial administration. However, at that moment,
India, written by John Strachey (Indian administrator)
was published. Harmand therefore decided to translate this
work rather than write a similar one, although his long
preface to the translation is quite a study in itself.

The value of this book for French administration of
Indochina was obvious to Harmand. At the very least it
would furnish the French with the essential elements
needed for success by demonstrating the "marvelous effects of administrative and financial autonomy" on the development of India and by showing all the advantages
which the mother country could derive from such a system.[81] Thus Harmand, like Chailley-Bert, believed in the
value of profiting from the experience of the English. He
contended, moreover, that the English had learned their
principles of domination of Asiatic peoples from Dupleix,
but, thanks to their perseverance, "the greatest of all their
qualities and one which can be called the first of all political virtues, they knew how to draw from the example of

Dupleix certain unseen consequences and had little by little perfected their methods." [82] Once the ethnic differences between India and Indochina were taken into consideration,[83] the methods evolved for India could be applied to the French possession in the same region.

India and Indochina had as a common basic characteristic the quality of being "possessions" and not "colonies." [84] Regions to be dominated and yet controlled in large measure by native administrations, they required a type of government entirely different from that of the ordinary colonies. Unfortunately, Harmand continued, the basic French colonial errors stemmed from ignorance of this fact and from the French tendency toward a type of centralization which grouped colonies and possessions under the same regime. A distinction between the two should have been discernible.

Colonies, stated Harmand, are regions which are susceptible to colonization and where the European finds similar conditions to those of his country of origin.[85] In such regions, the native is the human element of least importance in the development of the land, whereas the colonist is absolutely necessary. Furthermore, the colonist would there introduce his religion, his social habits, and other essential characteristics of the civilization of which he is a part, to such an extent that the colony would become a detached segment of the mother country and one in which a certain degree of assimilation would therefore be possible. Even so, Harmand believed the future of any colony was political independence.

Harmand gave the word "possession" a definition of

quite a different order.[86] Such territories, situated in already heavily populated tropical regions, only allowed the European to assume the role of director, of "protector of the native races."[87] The natives were the important element here; they were the ones who would improve the land by their own labor. With such improvement Harmand envisioned the subsequent economic prosperity of the possession, a state which would enable the necessary funds for local administration to come from local sources. In other words, the possessions would receive no direct subsidies from the mother country but would shoulder their own expenses, the virtue of British policy in India as Harmand interpreted it. Such a policy was the one he selected for Indochina because it would assure the administrative and financial autonomy he so ardently desired.

As regions of domination, possessions would have an administration different from that of France, and as the natives would therefore not be admitted to French citizenship, the colonial government would remain completely separated from the European administration. Thus representation in the parliament would be useless, if not harmful, as the British had previously recognized in India.[88] Basically, Harmand felt it necessary that the overseas possessions be organized as veritable states, endowed with all the features of such political units, but with one notable exception: the lack of political independence. Named "vice-kingdoms" by the English, such institutions, he thought, could possibly be called "vice-states" by the French.[89]

What Harmand and Chailley-Bert expressed were, for

the most part, more fully developed versions of ideas found scattered among the writings of many of the French imperialists of the day. Neither Harmand nor Chailley-Bert suggested slavish imitation of the British, but they did clearly emphasize that the French could learn something from their neighbors in colonial matters and could forget much of their own colonial past. With this the majority of imperialists would agree.

Yet it would be wrong to assume that Frenchmen, and colonial theorists in particular, were totally blind to some of the less attractive features of British imperial policy and were uncritical. Chailley-Bert, for one, acknowledged that the English had made more grave errors than the French, although he also insisted that the former had profited from theirs whereas the latter had not.[90] Rather than praise the British for their aloofness as many of his compatriots were wont to do, Emile Boutmy complained that the English never mixed with native populations nor attempted to conciliate them. They remained aloof, and oppressed, exploited, or even annihilated the native, he added.[91] Another author, Emile Baillaud, in his *La Politique indigène de l'Angleterre en Afrique occidentale*, criticized the British in this part of the world for their lack of uniformity in policy, adding that they should drop the fiction of the existence of independent tribes there.[92] And in his report to the Chamber of Deputies on the English colonies Deputy Maurice Ordinaire qualified otherwise unstinted praise for the English system by saying that the Englishman had respect for fundamental liberties "when he is not blinded by the conquering mania which makes him lose all sense of justice." [93]

But perhaps the most interesting, brief, critical analysis of the British colonial technique was made of India by Paul Bardoux, a professor at the Ecole des Sciences politiques, in his book *L'Angleterre radicale*. Bardoux wrote that if the economic growth of India proved to be the best justification of British imperialism, it would also prove to be its undoing. As a result of the economic stimulus provided by the British presence, both a native bourgeoisie and proletariat had developed: the bourgeoisie was ambitious for power; the proletariat, uprooted and poorly adjusted, was ideal prey for agitators.[94] To this situation was added another problem resulting from the British administration of India. In attempting to unify the various states of India in order to better administer and develop them, the British introduced the idea of unity to the Hindus and consequently awakened a sense of nationalism.[95] Still another serious disadvantage of the British rule in India, according to Bardoux, was the fact that India was "governed according to the system of Saint Moritz." [96] In retiring to the higher lands where veritable British cities were created, the British cut their ties with the growing urban proletariat at a time when its problems and needs should have been closely studied. All of these features led Bardoux to the conclusion that the British future in India would be grim.

Nevertheless, French imperialist opinion remained fixed in its advocacy of British methods. It is neither difficult to appreciate this view nor to understand why the Dutch were also looked upon with favor by French imperialists. Overseas possessions were justified primarily for practical reasons: growing industrial competition and concern over depression conditions stimulated interest in the search for new markets and new sources of raw materials. As the British and Dutch seemed to be ably handling their empires like good proprietors, admiration for their methods was understandable. British and Dutch colonial prosperity was thought to be the result of a sound native policy which necessitated the retention of native institutions, or, at least, their façade.

Current events seemed to do little to alter this opinion. The depression in the East Indies which began in 1895 and was largely responsible for the end of the economic liberalism practiced in this Dutch possession did not appear to cause the French any concern about their own evaluation of East Indian prosperity. The British setbacks in the Boer War also appeared to cause little concern. Not that some Frenchmen were unaware of the weakening of Britain's colonial position after the turn of the century. Victor Bérard, for instance, in his *L'Angleterre et l'impérialisme*, published in 1900, sensed a weakness of commercial origin in British colonial activities.[97] He considered English business conservatism and commercial insularity to be the causes of impending imperial decay. In an article appearing in the *Mercure de France*, it was claimed that Britain had overextended herself in her colonial empire, and this was the cause of her shaky world position in 1901.[98] But these were isolated worries; among the group of Frenchmen whose efforts were devoted to French imperial affairs few such examples come forth.

There was little change in the analyses of Dutch and British colonial methods in the decades of 1890 and 1900. And, indeed, there appeared to be little need for change in so far as foreign techniques could aid the French. Despite the ill effects of unfavorable economic development on the Dutch and the British, their colonial regions still seemed secure and the continuing source of economic return. That the age of colonial empires would so rapidly wane escaped the imagination of most French imperialists, although few among them believed the colonial relationship would remain static. Autonomy, even independence were envisioned for some future date, but economic interdependence was to continue and to be developed. To this end the Dutch and British seemed to be directing their efforts. They were business people whose colonial policy was declared to be realistic and sound.

From abroad, then, the French colonial theorists derived inspiration or, at least, guidance. As a result assimilation fared poorly as a colonial theory in the age of intensive imperialism. What the studies of comparative colonial systems seemed to prove, new interpretations of scientific and pseudoscientific theory also appeared to confirm.

Chapter 4

ASSIMILATION AND THE
SCIENTIFIC ATTITUDE

THE scientific attitude which became so widespread in the late nineteenth century gradually extended to colonial theory and altered it. In particular, the doctrine of evolution strongly influenced French colonial thought. Differences among races, the vast range of social and cultural attainments, and even the idea of the incompatibility of certain races with others were all emphasized, while these very issues became new and effective explanations for the difficulties of governing subject peoples and, moreover, the finest justifications for the rejection of the policy of assimilation.

French colonial theory of the period, permeated by evolutionary ideas, was slowly reformed. In place of the humanitarian notion of the basic equality of all peoples, colonial theorists now upheld the belief that certain important inequalities exist among races and peoples. Natural selection, as so interpreted, implied forward movement, social advancement. Affected by these thoughts, French theorists soon denied the possibility of assimilation and insisted on a policy in keeping with the discrepancies among human societies.

*French Interest in the Idea of Racial
and Social Variation*

Although such thought was new in colonial theory, the
tendency to stress the importance of the variety of human
development and of the inequalities existing among different peoples was noticeable in France at least from the
middle of the nineteenth century onward. Lamartine felt
that "the blood of the race always acts and manifests itself
after thousands of years on the physical forms and in the
moral habits of the family and the tribe." [1] The Comte de
Gobineau remarked in his long essay on the inequality of
races that "civilization is incommunicable." [2] And Renan,
in discussing linguistic differences, digressed momentarily
to affirm that "the march of humanity is not equal in all
regions: while noble races rise to sublime heights, lesser
races still rest in the humble regions which were their birth-
places." [3]

Moreover, on a broader scale, sociological research in
France raised the same problem by stimulating interest in
the variety of human species and by patiently seeking to
explain the reasons for this fact. Most notable in this endeavor was the Society of Anthropology, founded in 1859.
To a lesser degree the many geographical and colonial societies most active in colonial matters stimulated interest
through their various expeditions, conferences, and publications on French overseas regions and their different civilizations.

The full impact of this movement, however, was not felt

until quite late in the century and, of great importance, concomitantly with the interest in colonial theory.[4] During the last decades of the century, several highly reputable writers investigated and popularized some of the notions often included in the body of thought on social evolution and in this way provided the necessary arguments for an attack against the policy of assimilation, perhaps even unconsciously contributing to its cause.

As representatives of the then prevalent scientific trend, two men are worth singling out: Emile Durkheim and Alfred Fouillée. The former was a rising young sociologist soon to occupy a chair at the Sorbonne; the latter a member of the Institut de France, already well known for his stimulating books on philosophy and his articles on social psychology.[5]

In his *Règles de la méthode sociologique*, published in 1895, Durkheim undertook to explain the method by which variations in social development could be analyzed. His interpretation stressed the importance of social environment as a determinant of individual behavior. According to him, accepted group practices, which took the form of "social facts" in his vocabulary, largely guided the individual's actions in the society of which he was a part.[6] Society itself varied. Following Herbert Spencer's idea that social organisms grow from the simple to the complex by way of aggregation, Durkheim indicated the possible variety of resulting social phenomena and hence of social constitution.[7] The conclusion of his study was already offered in the preface when he wrote:

Our method . . . considers social facts as things the nature of which, no matter how supple and malleable, cannot be altered at will. How much more dangerous is the doctrine which imagines these facts to be only the product of mental combinations which a simple dialectical artifice can entirely change in an instant! [8]

Fouillée considered much the same problem. Concerned with the nature of national character and racial differences, he suggested the variety of human traits and abilities resulting directly from social differences; moreover, he indicated the almost insurmountable differences which hindered the alteration of these traits.

While he asserted that all of mankind had an initial common unity, he also declared that differences soon arose because of the processes of selection and heredity.[9] With the development of man in society, the "cerebral heritage" of individuals increased; not only did the brain become more highly developed prior to birth as a result of centuries of intellectual and social accumulation, but also it became more receptive after birth for the same reason.[10] In addition, mental perfectibility would increase according to the degree of perfection: the races already in the lead would continue to remain there.

In an illogical statement Fouillée said of the human races: "They might be compared to runners on the field of civilization: those who are ahead can run all the more quickly because their headstart is already greater." [11]

No one really lost, however, for Fouillée did see the possibility for improvement among the lesser races. He suggested two means by which this might be accomplished: education and intermarriage. About neither was he very enthusiastic.

Education, he thought, would be a very slow and difficult process by which to effect social change. Generations would be required and even then satisfactory results could not be guaranteed.[12] As for the ability of children to assimilate—to learn a language, for instance—Fouillée dismissed this as being only derived from an "intuition more or less spontaneous and close to instinct." To proceed beyond this stage of development would require a highly developed mentality, and "this is the particular heritage of civilization; it is the result of social selection which favors the minds that are better endowed." [13] Turning to Spencer as his authority, Fouillée asserted that less highly developed organisms require less time for development than more highly developed ones. The result is that "a heavier, more voluminous and complex brain requires more years for its complete development." [14]

The effects of intermarriage were analyzed with equal pessimism. Although Fouillée assumed that among the "subraces" in which variations would be slight—the white peoples of Europe, for instance—intermarriage would be salubrious, resulting in greater intellectual fecundity, he was certain that intermarriage among widely divergent peoples would be unhealthy, perhaps disastrous. "Unite a Bushman with a European woman and the struggle of antagonistic elements, instead of existing among diverse individuals, will

be transported to the character of the one and same individual. You would have a personality divided against itself, incoherent." [15]

Fouillée was not always so categorical about the nature
of the differences among peoples.[16] Nevertheless, he still
insisted that "national character is intimately connected to
temperament which itself is connected to inherited constitution and ethnic characteristics." [17]

Such prevalent sociological interpretations as these,[18]
translated into the language of French colonial theorists,
were to be of significance. They destroyed the belief in
the possibility of fusion between societies. The omnipotent
power of reason and the universal remedy of education
now appeared illusive. Henceforth, the doctrine of assimilation seemed to be founded on a mythical equality. Whether
the sociological views of the moment were entirely true or
not is of little concern here; [19] it is necessary to remember,
however, that many thinkers of the period considered them
scientifically irrefutable.

Soon French colonial theorists were interpreting the
processes of evolution as the salient reason for discarding
traditional colonial doctrine and for establishing a newer
theory in accord with the teachings of the day.

Gustave Le Bon, French Champion of Evolutionary Ideas

Even before Durkheim and Fouillée had penned their
words, Gustave Le Bon, one of those curious personalities
who, in the late nineteenth century, tried to embrace the

whole of knowledge, had established himself as one of the first and most ardent opponents of the Enlightenment idea of human equality and of the application of this idea to colonial policy in the guise of assimilation. Le Bon, above all others, contributed most directly to the supposedly scientific argumentation utilized for the "purification" of French colonial ideology. And his opinions, often categorical and sweeping, were greatly respected by many colonial theorists.

Le Bon was a prolific writer and a self-styled authority in many fields. A list of his books would run the gamut from horseback riding to mathematics and from the psychology of education to the civilization of the Arabs. At the peak of his career he was one of the most widely read French writers abroad, and his works were often translated into as many as eighteen languages. His well-known *mercredis* attracted a group of the famous which regularly included Aristide Briand and the Russian ambassador Izvolski.

Le Bon was a controversial figure.[20] Organized science in France often attacked him vigorously, denouncing the validity of his work; yet such notables as Henri Poincaré, Henri Bergson, and Daniel Berthelot continued to hold him in high esteem. Although he possessed no official title —and his enemies even begrudged him the honorific title of "doctor"—he assumed an important position among contemporary authorities in France. Moreover, the popularity and respect accorded him by the colonial theorists assured him an important voice in the criticism of doctrine.

Le Bon's particular interest centered around sociology and particularly on the problem of social variations among races. As early as 1881 he started to formulate his thought in a pretentious work entitled *L'Homme et les sociétés, leurs origines et leur histoire*. His objective was nothing less than a description of the creation and development of the universe, with a concomitant analysis of the laws which control the universe.[21] After a discussion of the various theories accounting for the creation of the world, he ventured into the delicate subject of "the character of the individual and of society." His goal, he avowed, was to refute the "most erroneous idea" that man is everywhere equal.[22]

Races manifest differences in their manners of thinking and of feeling, Le Bon declared. It is the national character of a people, "this community of sentiments developed in similar circumstances by the majority of individuals of a race,"[23] which is the basis of a people's customs and institutions. In addition, the inheritance of preceding generations plays a role of such great importance in the formation of one's character and personality that the individual is born, as it were, with an almost unchangeable psychological structure. Among peoples as well as among individuals, there is nothing more difficult to alter than character. In fine, the inequalities among peoples stem from the differences of social and intellectual development.

This idea is undoubtedly the key thought in Le Bon's most important and influential book, *Les Lois psychologiques de l'évolution des peuples*.[24] Herein he dogmatically affirmed that "each people possesses a constitution as fixed as its anatomical characteristics." [25] There is actually a national spirit gradually formed from the combination of a people's moral and intellectual characteristics and representing the synthesis of its past history and the influence of its ancestors.[26] While at first glance individuals may seem to vary considerably, Le Bon argued, closer observation proves that there are certain common "psychological characteristics" within a group which are reproduced constantly and regularly through heredity.[27]

The individual always remains representative of his race and is invariably affected by the invisible but powerful spirit of his people. Races themselves are permanent beings. Like the individual human organism which is composed of living cells that are constantly reproducing and dying, so a race is composed of individuals who perform a similar function.[28] The dead, like the living, leave their indelible mark on the character of their race. As a result of this slow process of racial development, the creation of national character requires considerable time.

Le Bon drew up a psychological classification of the human races, in which he distinguished four groups: primitive races, inferior races, intermediate races, and superior races. Confusion between these groups, he contended, is absolutely impossible, as the "mental gap which separates them is obvious." [29] While asserting that degrees of intelligence are the easy means by which differences among peoples may be discerned, he maintained that the nature of a people's character is more important. Group character, a combination of various popularly determined qualities, consists of such elements as perseverance, energy, self-mastery, and morality—the latter a "hereditary respect" for mores and customs.[30] If the cultural level of a race can be somewhat raised by means of education, its character remains fixed and unsusceptible to modification from without. And national character accounts for the grandeur and superiority of certain peoples, Le Bon added. Therefore, belief in the efficacy of education as a means of altering national habits and institutions is "one of the most harmful illusions that the theorists of pure reason have ever engendered."[31] And in colonial matters, "the application of the deductive system of our equalitarian ideas ruins metropolitan France and successively leads our colonies to a state of lamentable decadence."[32]

At the International Colonial Congress of 1889 Le Bon had already expressed these ideas, closely relating them to French colonial policy. Denouncing the policy of attempting to transform a people "à coup de décrets," he declared that every institutional system represents the needs of a particular people and, consequently, ought not to be changed.[33] Moreover, colonial powers were ridiculous in thinking that they could change institutions: social institutions result from a slow process of mental evolution which requires many centuries. In short, one "must consider as dangerous chimeras all our ideas of assimilating or Frenchifying any inferior people. Leave to the natives their customs, their institutions, their laws."[34]

The scientific antagonism toward assimilation was now

clearly expressed. Le Bon demonstrated to his own satisfaction the need to respect native institutions and to seek a
new and more scientific doctrine of colonial policy which
accorded with the facts. While much of what he solemnly
offered as "proof positive" would no longer be acceptable,
his ideas and others like them were soon to serve as the
basis of strong arguments against the policy of assimilation.

Yet it appeared that the direct influence of sociological
doctrine on French colonial policy was initially rather
slow. Not until the waning years of the nineteenth century
did it become widely felt.

A New Criticism of Assimilation

In 1899 the efforts started by Le Bon were resumed and
in a most dramatic fashion. In that year *La Psychologie de
la colonisation française dans ses rapports avec les sociétés
indigènes* by Léopold de Saussure appeared. Saussure, a
naval lieutenant of little previous renown who had studied
native customs while doing service in the Far East, soon
gained an enthusiastic audience.[35]

The volume is interesting, if often pseudoscientific. Its
appearance was very timely. Saussure had deferred its publication for some time because he felt that the ideas contained in it were most unpopular. However, the results of
the Spanish-American War seemed to offer tangible and
contemporary proof of what he contended;[36] the book
was then published.

The Spanish-American War was ominous to Saussure, a

stark revelation of what could happen to colonial nations bent upon assimilating native populations. After centuries of religious assimilation Cuba and the Philippines violently broke away from their mother country, and in the Philippines members of the clergy were driven out and even persecuted. Obviously, the unreasonable contemporary colonial policy pursued by Spain was the principal cause for these successful revolutions, but in Saussure's eyes the outbreak and the outcome were grim proof of the inevitable results of the old Spanish policy of assimilation.[37] The assimilative tendency of "Latin races" appeared to be harmful whether it was of a religious nature, as that of Spain, or of a political and social nature, as that of France. Comparing Spanish colonial policy with that of the French, he warned: "When the occasion arises, we will see similar results in our own endeavors." [38] The French system had to be changed, and in order to do so, the national "dogmas" which directed French colonial policy had to be analyzed; hence, the criticism of assimilation.

La Psychologie de la colonisation française was a strong attack on French policy. Largely supported by the ideas of Le Bon, whose contribution he happily acknowledged, Saussure denounced assimilation with an ardor hitherto unknown.

The particular problem of French colonialism as he saw it stemmed from the very nature of French colonial policy which he believed was "fatally imposed on us by hereditary sentiment, beliefs, and concepts which are part of our national character." [39] The two important elements which colored this policy were belief in the unity of mankind and belief in the efficacy of pure reason, both of which ran counter to the laws of evolution.

Races as well as species are formed by a "hereditary accumulation of imperceptible changes." [40] From their origins the human races began to diverge and are hence presently separated by anatomical and mental characteristics which are fixed and which are transmittible to other races only after the lapse of considerable time. [41] The characteristics of any civilization are manifestations of racial character; therefore, acquisition of a foreign culture presupposes acquisition of certain mental traits. [42] Race as used here by Saussure meant "psychological race" which is distinguishable by mental characteristics slowly acquired over a determined period of history. [43] Social institutions, beliefs, language and the like are the outward manifestations of such a race. All of this meant to Saussure what it meant to Le Bon: the explosion of the myth of natural equality among races. [44]

Yet French colonial doctrine was opposed to this teaching, Saussure obviously felt, because of its philosophical origins. These he traced back to the philosophy of the eighteenth century at which time man was reduced to a "mathematical unit" supposedly similar everywhere. [45] Little by little the abstract idea of the universality of mankind began to penetrate the intellectual life of Europe and soon became a new secular religion. The result was all human activity was thereafter guided along abstract principles and this, in turn, only led to a decided tendency to ignore the important results of pragmatic experience. Although the eighteenth-century principles, enthusiastically applied during the Revolution, were no longer believed in wholeheartedly as a solution to national problems, the temptation to apply them to native societies was irresistible. The unfortunate outcome of this practice was the conflict between principles and realities which shook the entire French colonial structure.[46]

This conflict was, according to Saussure, the very crux of French colonial confusion and accounted for the difficulties facing France in her colonies. Although he believed that a colonial power could direct her colonies toward improvement in accordance with their own needs and interests, he firmly denied that this could be accomplished by assimilation which, in itself, implied a total transformation of native social structure.[47] As it is a purely abstract doctrine, assimilation could not be limited solely to changes within the framework of existing native institutions but would necessitate the erection of an entirely new system. Yet such a goal could never be attained if only because of obvious native opposition to it and because of the continually vexing problem of insufficient financial allocations for its realization.

Wherever and however practiced, therefore, assimilation would have the same disastrous effects. In those regions endowed with highly developed societies, native resentment would naturally be felt as a result of the destruction of the respected local institutions; in countries of mixed populations, assimilation would result in local representation in the French parliament, a fact which implied that the *créoles* would exercise an unhealthy influence on the formulation of colonial policy.[48] Everywhere, Saussure concluded, assimilative measures provoked "disorganization, financial deficit, and a lowering of morality." [49]

To dissipate any illusions that one might have had about the apparent success of Western assimilation by Japan, Saussure pointed out that the only true transformation made in that country was of a material nature. Japanese mental and moral character was not changed in any respect and, what is more, the Japanese firmly resisted any such changes.[50] Yet the instance of Japan led Saussure to an important conclusion: colonial peoples could profit from material progress as much as Europeans. The error made by the French in their colonies was to think that only after the minds of the people had been assimilated could material development succeed. Ironically, Saussure lamented, "this sterile and costly attempt at mental assimilation" has hindered the economic development of the colonies.[51]

No doubt in an attempt to bolster his arguments further and to show that the French were misguided in their views of the Romans, Saussure drew certain conclusions from the colonial practices of two other peoples: the British and the Romans. He was impressed by the English effort in India, which he felt bore strong resemblance to that of the Romans in Gaul. Above all, he noted that both peoples had similar qualities: a practical sense and a sense of reality.[52]

Both assured the success of their conquests by obtaining the cooperation of the natives. Local institutions and beliefs were respected, and development of the countries was achieved by their own means.

The major difference between the English and the French systems was obvious to Saussure. The basis of the former was "derived only from experience," while the basis of the latter was founded "on a dogma and on the faith it inspired in an entire people." [53] In effect, this dogma resulted from a sentiment peculiar to France: classical Latinism. Difficult to define, it consisted, nevertheless, in a taste for simplicity and uniformity. "Born out of certain elements in the Judaic and Roman traditions, cultivated by the monarchy, it has become in France a mental habit, an inherited ideal and one of the principal characteristics of the race." [54]

This brief passage summarized the essential psychological problem which, in Saussure's eyes, confronted French colonial affairs. Considering the much-vaunted Latin spirit as something of a *mystique*, Saussure all but despaired of the possibility of modifying it. Only by a slow, tedious transformation of national character could this be accomplished. Thinking in this fashion, Saussure was bound to be very pessimistic about the chances of discarding the doctrine of assimilation. He concluded that the partisans of the traditional policy would once again succeed in assuring its primacy by convincing the next colonial congress, scheduled for 1900, of its value.[55] On this point, however, he was wrong.

Acceptance of the Evolutionary Theories

From the opening of the first session of the International Congress of Colonial Sociology, convoked on the occasion of the Great International Exposition of 1900 at Paris for the purpose of studying native problems, one theme for discussion was very evident: denunciation of assimilation. "To try to assimilate the natives would be a great folly," [56] proclaimed H. Van Kol, the Dutch representative. C. Marchal, deputy from Algeria, exclaimed: "No assimilation! This is the formula, I believe, which ought to be inscribed on the threshold of a program of colonial law." [57] Furthermore, Marchal denounced "the literary autosuggestion which leads our Latin spirits to see all of life in a system of education or in institutions already made." [58] And Arthur Girault, Professor of Law at the University of Poitiers, who but a few years before had subscribed to assimilation,[59] now changed his views and insisted upon the maintenance of native institutions. "These institutions are, in effect, in harmony with the social state of the natives, with their economic needs, with their moral and religious conceptions." [60]

In a lengthy paper to the Congress, Auguste Billiard, administrator of a mixed commune in Algeria, wrote of the evil effects of assimilation.[61] Comparing the world of man with the vegetable kingdom, he remarked that the former is also divided into various zones "susceptible to the flourishing of different mentalities." [62] Consequently, foreign institutions wherever introduced could not take root and would only disturb the native populations. But this was not the only possible bad effect of assimilation. If the assimilated colony should be granted a large amount of autonomy, the colonists, perhaps humiliated by their assimilation with an inferior race, would erect social barriers between themselves and the natives. A situation such as that in the south of the United States might easily result, Billiard cautioned.[63] Or again, perhaps directly attached to the mother country, the colony might obtain the right of representation in the national parliament. Its deputies would thereupon demand representation in proportion to the number of their electors, an event which could only result in a minority position for the metropolitan representation. From these arguments, Billiard concluded that "a sincere renunciation of all attempts of assimilation" was absolutely necessary.[64]

Behind the remarks made by the various participants at the congress can at last be seen the influence of the social sciences, particularly of sociology—as the name of the congress would indicate. The seeds planted by Le Bon and others had finally taken root, grown, and were now bearing fruit. The law of evolution, variously interpreted, was the central argument invoked to reject assimilation and to assure respect of native institutions. Perhaps one can best sum up the sentiments of the majority of the members of the congress in the words of one member: "A race can no more be assimilated than metals can be transmuted." [65]

It is not surprising, therefore, that the results of the congress indicated to French imperialists that the assimilative spirit was now apparently dead, at least in doctrine. The

Congress of 1900 adopted by unanimous vote the resolution that local administrative organisms should be maintained. It also adopted the resolution that native institutions and customs should be respected as far as possible; and, finally, it affirmed that native education should be geared to the needs of the local inhabitants.[66]

With amazing rapidity, the ideological structure upon which French colonial practice had been avowedly based appeared to collapse. The voices heretofore openly advocating assimilation were silenced; the cherished ideas inherited from the *philosophes* were cast aside. The newly vaunted scientific attitude toward colonial problems had now gained sway and was assumed by nearly all of the colonial writers of the period. A realistic colonial policy based on current scientific precepts was henceforth demanded.[67] Paul Leroy-Beaulieu pointed out that "colonial sociology" was unknown even a quarter of a century before.[68] Now, he affirmed, in place of the older haphazard method, a "collection of observations and precepts for the equitable and efficacious treatment of native races in the colonies," [69] was becoming a guide for colonial policy.

Colonial practice was to be based on empirical evidence. Observation, investigation, analysis became the key words used. The new arguments may be summarized by paraphrasing the words of F. J. Clozel, who himself carefully investigated the customs of the natives of the Ivory Coast. Men are not abstractions; they live in their time and place and are affected by their past and their environment. In order to govern any of the colonies, the French should acquire a thorough knowledge of the particular region with a view to understanding its ethnological make-up.[70] Or, as another writer aptly said—making use of an analogy to a mechanical device then as tricky to run as a new colony— no automobile owner would undertake to drive his machine without first being thoroughly acquainted with it; in like manner, the colonizing nation must first understand her colonies before seeking to utilize them.[71]

Of chief concern to the colonial theorists now interested in the renovation of native policy were the problems presented by Le Bon and Fouillée and stressed at the colonial congress of 1900. Almost everyone conceded that psychological influences and sociological variations rendered the task of administering and developing a colonial region difficult. Foreign mentalities were indeed thought of as being as far apart and as dissimilar as the geographical regions in which they flourished. Or, to change the simile to one the theorists themselves might have used, the mentalities within the colonial empire were often as widely separated as those of children and adults.[72] To this was added the thought that the primitive mind was totally different from the civilized one, was impenetrable and unassimilable. Theorists now also assumed that local customs and institutions were in some way the "natural rights" of the natives and consequently had to be respected.[73] And it was said that the French had not understood the significance of the fact that it was collectivities with their own institutions and not individuals that were being colonized.[74]

In his study, *De l'éducation des races*, Paul Giran, ad-

ministrator of civil services in Indochina, emphasized most
of these prevalent ideas. Like others before him, he strongly
relied on the concept of organic development of societies as
explained by Gustave Le Bon, to whom, incidentally, he
also indicated his indebtedness. There is no need to re-
capitulate here Giran's arguments on the subject, for they
run parallel with those of Saussure and, in turn, with those
of Le Bon. What gives Giran's work its interest is the underlying assertion that a need exists to distinguish between
two existing forms of education. Of these two types, described by Giran as the sociological or collective and the
psychological or individual, only the former had any place
in colonial affairs.[75] Individual education involved a grave
danger which took the form of *éducationisme*, a concept
which Giran defined as the belief in the omnipotence of
education. "The individual is for the educationist an abstract unit, part of an abstract whole," [76] hence one and
the same everywhere regardless of prevailing conditions.
Giran insisted that the idea of assimilation had issued from
this "nefarious theory." [77] But thanks to the results of
sociology the ideas cherished by the educationists were
falling into decay and were being replaced by the idea of
sociological or collective education. This latter concept,
Giran assumed, developed from the basic premise that education was a social function changing according to environment and embodying a particular collective ideal
rather than an individual or universal one.[78] In short, education reflected the social views and objectives of a given
society. While the realization of this fact did not destroy

the possibility of the education of a more backward race
by a more advanced one, it did mean this education would
have to proceed slowly and cautiously. To Giran, indirect
action on the environment rather than direct action on the
individual would best achieve desired changes in the race,
for social sentiments and habits—the reflection of the environment—would then change.[79] For instance, the betterment of health standards and economic conditions would
lead to social and cultural betterment.

In the thoughts of Giran and those of the other Frenchmen examined above, the great importance of evolutionary
ideas is clearly found. Regardless of the manner in which
they were used, these ideas did have a salubrious effect on
the development of French colonial theory. Aside from
leading to much needed introspection concerning colonial
administration, they also placed the anticipated results of
colonial activity in better perspective. The bountiful re-
wards of either a material or of a spiritual nature which
had been held out to the French people in order to win
them over to the colonial cause were no longer expected
immediately or even in the near future.

A good example of this trend of thought can be found
in the writing of Leroy-Beaulieu, whose arguments em-
phasizing the economic need of the colonies had become
classic. He, too, embraced evolutionary thought in fact if
not in name. The sixth edition of his great work on
colonization clearly indicated that overseas ventures
promised their greatest results in the distant future. He still
insisted that the work of economic development had to be

commenced immediately and to this end the native, introduced to some European ways, would be a most valuable
ally.[80] Yet in order that such economic cooperation could
be guaranteed under satisfactory conditions, the mental and
material amelioration of the native would be required. Such
development could not be obtained in a few generations,
Leroy-Beaulieu gravely wrote, but would have to be slowly
wrought over a period of time one or two centuries long
"so that the action on the mental and spiritual state of
primitive populations would have a general and profound
effect." [81]

Henceforth, the nation's civilizing mission was to be fulfilled in conformity with the ideas expressed by contemporary sociologists. It was soon generally believed that the
advantages of Western civilization, instead of being useful
to colonial populations, could well be harmful.[82] As a result of this assertion, it was thought necessary to proceed
initially and most cautiously with the material betterment
of these populations and to avoid any precipitious introduction of French cultural benefits. One critic declared
that the actions of primitive peoples should not be judged
"with the mentality of a subtle and enlightened Parisian." [83]
Another condemned any move toward assimilation of local
administration as ridiculous and went so far as to insist that
the imposition of French legislation and judicial organization would not only destroy the basic social relationships
of the natives but would also more than likely provoke
revolution.[84]

To some writers interested in evolutionary doctrine as it

was related to primitive societies, the nature of the *âme noire* was particularly fascinating. Perhaps the vastness and mystery of the recent French acquisitions in west and equitorial Africa intrigued the imperialists of the time and aroused in them a particular interest in the strange and the unknown of Darkest Africa. Indeed, the sparse native populations of Africa readily attracted study and investigation. Here were societies which were seemingly completely divorced from Western civilization and most unlike the other French colonial populations who either had a civilization readily appreciated by the European or who at least retained some visible signs of former greatness. Le Bon had placed these African populations in the "inferior race" category he had devised. In his eyes, they were capable of grasping the rudiments of civilization but the rudiments only.[85] Other writers were enticed by what they described as the simplicity and child-like attitude of the colored peoples.

The negro spirit is something like the spirit of our first ancestors. It is unpolished and crude, but its freshness is without comparison. In coming into contact with it, one feels humble but also immersed in the very sources of human sensitivity. Singular antithesis, this contact makes one at the same time less proud and more virile! [86]

For Commandant Edmond Ferry, the Sudanese, although not savages, were close enough to manifest the primitive state's most significant characteristics.[87] The Sudanese, in his view, were in their unhappy condition as the result of centuries of barbarism, of wars, and of slavery. However, the fortunes of civilization could be brought to these peoples; yet before this goal could be achieved, the population would have to pass through the different stages of civilization in the same way as other peoples before them. The French role in this evolutionary struggle was to aid the native "in this long and difficult climb toward the good and the beautiful." [88]

In a very similar vein Clozel stressed the fact that the French had some thirty centuries of civilization behind them.[89] For this reason the African peoples of the French empire could not be expected to travel in one day the long road that the French had slowly followed. Nor would it even be advisable to attempt to make the native populations over in the European image. Only a caricature would result from such an attempt, as the Republics of Haiti and Liberia had clearly shown.[90] Clozel concluded that African institutions be accepted as they were, with French efforts being channeled in the direction of the natural development of these institutions.

On all sides and apparently on all accounts then, the doctrinal dispute over assimilation was waged in the name of social science. Assimilation was scourged, while the new precepts of colonial sociology were warmly welcomed. If the imperialists as denouncers of assimilation could cry: "assimilation is nonsense, a stupidity which can only cause deceptions and difficulties," [91] as proud exponents of colonial sociology they could exclaim, amid applause, "the law of evolution imposes itself on colonial policy." [92]

What was deemed scientific doctrine, it would thus

seem, rendered good service to the colonial theorists who sought revision of policy and doctrine. The *esprit de système* cherished by the French and transformed by them into colonial assimilation was weakened if not destroyed. Yet the advocacy of a more realistic and rational policy meant that the egalitarian ideas which gave French colonization in theory, at least, its ennobling character were now in desuetude.

Negative Aspects of Evolutionary Thought

The various interpretations of evolution offered by the French may well have served the colonial cause by leading to a new sort of colonial policy which assured respect for native institutions. But these interpretations did have their unfavorable aspects as well. A type of ethnocentrism was manifested by a goodly number of French writers. All colonial problems were still judged strictly from the European point of view. The "colonial situation" which ensued when European and native met not infrequently led the European, too often an untrained observer, to disparage what he saw, to consider abnormal what he did not understand.[93] The native, whether Annamite or Touareg, was viewed in a condescending or paternalistic fashion. Moreover, too few of the so-called scientific authorities had personally studied the populations about which they freely wrote. Much theory was based on secondhand and frequently unreliable observations. Then, the classification of races, as the work of Gustave Le Bon has shown, was easily made and rigidly fixed. As a result, certain peoples were placed in a lowly position from which collective escape seemed impossible. Called inferior and backward, these peoples, notably the Africans, were destined to remain in an almost uncivilized state for many centuries, according to some French writers.[94] The law of evolution was invoked as a guarantee of this status. Yet such conclusions are understandable if viewed from the historical period in which Social Darwinism was offered as a self-evident truth. At least two French writers nevertheless feared a racial smugness which they felt was in the making, even if not openly admitted or consciously felt. Although the writings of these two men were not part of the mainstream of contemporary imperialist thought and probably did not even momentarily affect the flow of that stream, they should be mentioned if for no other reason than to indicate the dangers inherent in the popular thinking of the day.

Pierre Mille and Marius-Ary Le Blond were recognized literary figures and could claim an affinity for the colonial cause through the novels they had written about colonial life.[95] In the two articles which appeared in the *Revue de Paris*—Mille's "La Race supérieure" [96] and Le Blond's "La Race inférieure" [97]—both authors were desirous of exploding a myth they thought was beginning to flourish in France.[98]

Mille stated that the current justification for colonial expansion was belief in the racial superiority of the white man. Yet he recognized that this belief was not new; on

the contrary it had traversed three periods: first, when the
Europeans felt the need to spread the Christian faith during the first period of their overseas expansion; second,
when the belief in reason replaced Christian proselytism and
led the European to assume a moral superiority; and finally,
the period in which Mille was writing.[99]

The contemporary white man believed in the incontest-
able superiority of his brain. This superiority, Mille continued, led to the further belief that the white man had a
right to establish an imperium over the nonwhite peoples.
Scientific discoveries and technological advancements were
greatly responsible for the new "dogma." The thought expressed during the reign of Louis XV that the French were
inferior to other peoples, especially the Chinese, had completely changed.

A century later, the scientists who have replaced the Jesuits and
the philosophers in the confidence of the people, profess with
the same assurance that the Chinese, having no railroads, no
mechanical textile machinery, no Napoleon and no Moltke are
extremely inferior to us. Some facts derived from direct observation and the diffusion of Darwinian theories have strength-
ened this observation.[100]

The white man was now acclaimed to be the one who syn-
thesized the best, who had the best sense of organization,
of leadership, of justice. He progressed while other races
remained static.

Mille admitted that an examination of the conditions of
the Arab, Berber, and colored races did favor the argument of white racial superiority. But the Asiatic races pre-

sented a problem to the theorists who, still affirming the intellectual superiority of the white race, sought a new base from which to argue. It was the "utilitarian economists" who were responsible for the new argument.[101] Considering the material well-being of mankind an important condition, they insisted that humanity, of necessity, should exploit the natural resources of the world. Those peoples who had done little or nothing to make use of their resources might well be expelled or at least subjugated. If this argument did not include racial superiority *ipso facto,* Mille wrote, belief that the Europeans were the only peoples capable of the necessary exploitation soon led to such a sentiment. But the successful material advancement and the excellent development of natural resources by the Japanese destroyed this whole argument of white superiority.[102]

Le Blond was primarily concerned about the ideas of racial inferiority as applied to the Negro. He assailed the American prejudice against the Negro and the supposed justification of it by reference to Biblical quotations.[103] He also attacked the more subtle arguments about Negro inferiority which he found in the writings of Renan and Gobineau. Moreover, he was concerned about Saussure's book and its wide acceptance by serious writers.[104] In his view, the same prejudices, the same instincts toward racial subservience and exploitation were to be found behind writings of this sort as were to be found in the use made of Biblical quotations in America.

The Negroes were not by nature inferior. What arrested

their psychological development had been the excessive ease of their material life. However, every time that these peoples are found in normal living conditions, or every time that they come in contact with advanced civilizations, they prove themselves "perfectible." [105] And Le Blond concluded that the Negro race "has conducted itself in relation to the land and climate in which it lives with as much industry as other human races have in their regions." [106]

While the observations of Mille and Le Blond have since been borne out in large measure, the obvious problems resulting from belief in racial superiority were scarcely observed by the imperialist theorists in France. On the whole, only the positive interpretations of the importance of the social sciences as related to colonial policy attracted attention. To a great extent they stimulated field studies on indigenous conditions in the colonial areas. At the International Congress of Ethnographic Sciences held in Paris in 1902 and at the French Colonial Congresses meeting between 1904 and 1908, the papers on native customs and habits were profuse in number. In fact, as part of the annual French Colonial Congress a section devoted to sociology and ethnography was begun with the 1906 congress and headed by Réné Worms, editor of the *Revue internationale de sociologie*. Its self-appointed task was the study of the various native populations comprising the French Empire. In 1906, for instance, it studied Madagascar; 1907, Laos and Cambodia; 1908, Annam. Moreover, the missions sent to Africa by the government and by such institutions as the Comité de l'Afrique française reported back any number of interesting facts on native societies. Although most of the fruitful studies were not produced until after the First World War, the initial efforts made before then were highly laudable. Here seemed to be practical confirmation of the new but hitherto untried theories concerning social development, the impact of cultures, the variations of mankind.

Chapter 5

IMPERIALISM: EXPRESSION OF MAN'S
WILL TO POWER

THE interest which French theorists of imperialism manifested in current evolutionary concepts was intensified by those writers who questioned the value of French colonial doctrine on the grounds that it was not in keeping with the basic characteristic of human nature: man's aggressiveness. These individuals contended that equality and humanitarianism could scarcely play a role where force alone abided. Colonial aggrandizement was achieved by force and this achievement had to be maintained by force; such was the essence of their argument. Ideas of this sort seemed particularly plausible at the time because man's supposedly bellicose spirit was everywhere being emphasized, even lauded, to the detriment of eighteenth-century humanitarianism, the intellectual basis of assimilation.

By the end of the nineteenth century a growing literature concerning the importance of brute force as an essential factor in all human activity was being widely read and accepted. Most of the theoretical arguments upon which the French imperialists interested in the idea of force based their own statements had already been popularized. Although the interpretation of biological evolutionary theory in terms of the social sciences certainly led to gross distortions,[1] this growing doctrine of force, given currency by people running the gamut from Ruskin to Moltke, seemed to sweep over Europe in reckless fashion.

Outside France dominant figures like Nietzsche and Spencer, and lesser, but equally interesting personages like the Russian sociologist Novicow, the Polish sociologist Gumplowicz and the Italian sociologist Vaccaro were enjoying substantial popularity, their own ideas being welcomed in France. While Nietzsche's notion of the will to power and Spencer's popular concepts of the survival of the fittest led many people to conceive of life as a struggle and of nature as aggressive activity, the sociological interpretations of Gumplowicz and Vaccaro also lent weight to the assertion that the organization and expansion of society were the direct results of this never-ending struggle among people and races.[2] Novicow, whose writings were accorded as great respect in French sociological circles as those of Spencer,[3] moved along similar lines. Although later his ardor for the idea of struggle and survival expressed in Spencerian terms cooled considerably, in early works it was intense. His *Politique internationale* considered international relations "the art of conducting the struggle for existence between social organisms;"[4] his *Les Luttes entre sociétés humaines* considered the whole universe from macrocosm to microcosm as being engaged in an intricate but never-ending struggle: "In a general sense the universe is the theatre of chemical, astronomical, geo-

logical, biological, psychological and social struggles." [5]
No more sweeping statement than this last is to be found
in the literature of the time.

Within France itself the ever-active Gustave Le Bon explained his views on force while discussing the importance
of the law of evolution as a determinant in history. Rei-
terating what Spencer had already popularized, Le Bon
declared that the struggle for existence had been inces-
sant and unavoidable throughout the history of humanity.[6]
In fact he believed this struggle to be the natural and permanent state of man as well as of animals.[7] It also was the
most decisive factor in progress, for it required societies
and individuals to advance or else to be crushed under foot
by their more ardent and ambitious rivals. In this world,
he contended, there is only one true, natural law, and it
is the right of the strongest.[8] "The right of the strongest!
It is in vain that the humanitarian philosophers from the
depths of their studies would contest its potency. It is the
only law which always imposes itself, and it is also the one
which has made humanity progress the most." [9]

No one in France tried with more effort to analyze all
the divergent ideas about the nature and use of force than
did Ernest Seillière, sociologist and philosopher. In his long
work *Philosophie de l'impérialisme*,[10] he undertook the explanation of imperialism as an all pervasive force and one
observable in the writings of people like Gobineau, Nietzsche, and even Rousseau.

It was from Nietzsche that Seillière borrowed his definition of imperialism. He thought that imperialism best
expressed the idea of the will to power.[11] Whether felt by

individuals, as Nietzsche explained it, or by groups and classes, as Gobineau and Rousseau would have it, the primordial need for self-assertion and communal expansion as a means of survival and of the assurance of future well-being was expressed through the exercise of power.[12] Seillière insisted particularly on the utilitarian aspects of imperialism and more often than not referred to these as "imperialistic utilitarianism." The idea was neither original nor exciting. As Seillière explained it, men, organized into clans and societies, became warlike groups to assure better success in their forceful incursions. In effect a contract between warriors and chiefs—the idea of the Germanic *comitatus*, so well explained by Tacitus—was formed which Seillière saw as the root of "imperialistic utilitarianism." [13] Thus imperialism, man's expansionist tendency, became a group activity cordinated in order to guarantee the future well-being of the society concerned.

The possible excesses of imperialism, however, were reduced as man made use of his accumulated past experiences and as society grew more complex. Although man realized that the use of force was a means by which to guarantee the continuance of his personal and collective life, he also realized that force, if abused, could ultimately be disastrous. The very nature of imperialism, therefore, led to the creation of morality and law, for relations between individuals and societies had to be regulated by mutual agreement if imperialism was to be kept in check.[14] As a result another type of imperialism evolved, and this was called "rational" by Seillière.

Rational imperialism developed as new social influences

came to bear. In his own day Seillière noted that democratic imperialism held sway: the people were in control.
The struggle between unbridled and controlled imperialism, between force and reason, continued, but Seillière's
hope was centered on the belief that force would eventually be subordinated to reason so that a more equitable
world would appear.[15]

These brief statements of Seillière's ideas on imperialism
indicate the correlation which was being made between
imperialism and force. Among the colonial theorists in
France the role of force in imperialism had long been acknowledged but had never been used as an argument for or
against any particular colonial doctrine. It was generally
invoked merely as a justification for overseas expansion.

Since the beginning of the Third Republic, French imperialists had tried to demonstrate to their compatriots that
the conquest and annexation of underdeveloped regions was
in the logic of things. The idea of the survival of the fittest
and the struggle it implied was made one of the major
reasons for concern over the apparently limited economic
resources of the world. Overseas expansion was considered
obligatory for any nation wishing to assure its share of these
resources. Even though this economic argument in favor of
expansion had been used by Jules Ferry and Leroy-Beaulieu, among others, in the 1880's, it was still one of the
standard arguments in the 1890's. Scarcely any ardent imperialist intent upon justifying France's overseas empire
passed up the opportunity to have his say on the economic
necessity of colonies. The example of Arthur Girault is a

good one, particularly as his basic work on colonial policy enjoyed an ever-growing reputation.[16]

Girault desired to show that expansion was a natural thing. In order to do so he lashed out against the opponents of imperialism who claimed that equality exists among races and, as a result, affirmed no one race had the right to interfere with the activities of another. This argument was specious, insisted Girault. In his opinion no race had the right to refuse economic intercourse with others, nor did it have the right to leave its land undeveloped.[17] On the contrary, it is a "natural and higher law" that all peoples are to obtain by work or trade all products available on the earth.[18]

In certain instances, however, native peoples do not know how to utilize the wealth about them and invariably hinder others more capable than themselves from enjoying it. Rousseau's noble savage uncorrupted by civilization should not be allowed to prevail where such conditions exist, Girault declared. Rather the law of natural selection must play its part unhindered.

There is a law common not only to the human species but also to all living things that individuals less well endowed disappear before those better endowed. The progressive extinction of inferior races by civilized ones, or, if one does not like these words, the destruction of the weak by the strong, is the very condition of progress.[19]

Girault's interpretation of the aggressive nature of economic competition was shared by most French imperialists and, indeed, most European imperialists who seized upon this argument for their own purposes. In addition to this popular economic interpretation, there was another one which concerned political matters.

The highly competitive aspect of nationalism in the late nineteenth century seemed to prove that only great and fit nations would survive. The Prussian victory over France in 1870 had driven this thought home to the French.[20] Now the words of Prévost-Paradol concerning the insecurity of France's future without a policy of overseas expansion seemed prophetic.[21] There was wide agreement among the imperialists that France would readily lose her standing as a world power if she remained solely confined to her continental limits. Under such conditions, one writer insisted, any nation would be "condemned to misery, internecine struggles, to base passions and decadence." [22] Another author imagined a noncolonial France as only a large Switzerland.[23] But it was Chailley-Bert who most dramatically underlined the purpose of France's colonial policy:

It is the protest against a menacing future; it is the affirmation of a great people who are aware of their position in the world and also of the great services they render to the world. If France disappeared there would be less justice and enlightenment in the world. France has a feeling for such things. She must live; she must act. Hence, a new orientation of her policies.[24]

Yet, stripped of their patriotic language, all such arguments were basically justifications for imperialism and the aggressiveness it implied. They did not affect colonial policy as such. When force and aggression were explained

as the essential factors which should determine native
policy, however, a new interpretation of colonial theory
arose which changed the Frenchman from a cultural mis-
sionary into a kind tyrant at best. Two authors in particular subscribed to this idea and showed that assimilation was
untenable in face of it. They were Charles Régismanset and
Jules Harmand.

The Ideas of Charles Régismanset

No writer in this period was a more bitter critic of the
intellectual bases of French colonial doctrine, as well as
those of all colonial theories, than was Charles Régismanset.
After the First World War he was Director of Economic
Affairs in the Ministry of Commerce and, curiously, a
champion of assimilation; [25] in the opening years of the
century he was desirous of removing all justifications from
imperialism and of revealing it as he saw it: the result of
naked force.

Quite unlike most of his contemporaries Régismanset did
not believe colonization to be a science. To him all colonial
activity was a social fact which found its sole cause in the
active life of man; in turn, all of man's activity was manifested by force. This is the essential thesis of the small
book Régismanset wrote under the pseudonym of Charles
Siger: *Essai sur la colonisation.*[26]

In a philosophical tone much in keeping with contemporary thought, he emphasized the role of force in life in
general and in colonialism in particular. Life is activity, he

said; it can be nothing else: "fatal activity, universal activity, such is the law." [27] This activity can only express itself by force; no other means exists.[28] Hence colonization, as a form of universal activity, is itself but a manifestation of force. This point Régismanset belabored by analyzing the history of colonial expansion as a series of acts in which the stronger party expropriates the land of the weaker.[29] His conclusion is a reiteration of his basic premise: "Without force, no colonization. That is the law." [30]

As this idea of human activity is, however, a general and abstract one, to be realized it must be diversified into concrete and easily appreciated motivations.[31] The intelligence of the average person requires something far more comprehensible than the purely intellectual notion of activity. Just as beauty is an abstract idea needing to be translated into specific types, so the abstract idea of activity is in need of particular motivation. Now the motivations for mass exodus or colonial expansion can readily be placed into two general categories: the one material or economic, the other psychological.[32] The former includes such things as overpopulation, poor climate, the need for new markets. The latter consists of the native curiosity of man, the spirit of adventure, and personal ambition. All are, according to Régismanset, but various means of expressing human activity.

Yet because mundane, daily existence and the struggles it entails scarcely satisfy man, he invents motives for his basic actions. The world which man has created is not enough. He insists upon arranging his creation, almost as if he were suddenly afraid he was no longer its master.

Like the architect who destroys the lines of his structure with distracting decoration in order to show he is the creator of it, man must invent motives for his every action.[33]

Although religion is, in Régismanset's eyes, the most ingenious pretext conceived by man to justify expansion, the motive he singled out for particularly vehement criticism is humanitarianism. The "pus which is discharged from the canker of practical reason," [34] humanitarianism is also to be classified as a new sort of religion. Its ideal is the Christian one but deformed by a rationalist interpretation so that the result is really a parody of religion. Nevertheless, in its initial development, humanitarianism did have a certain laudable quality: disinterestedness. Then in the eighteenth century humanitarianism became a pretext for overseas expansion and thereafter could be considered in no way commendable. For this devious use the British were chiefly responsible. They annexed territory under the guise of helping the natives, of assuring internal peace.[35]

The French, however, never got beyond the stage of disinterested humanitarianism. Certain self-styled French prophets even wanted to make this form of humanitarianism the true motive for French colonization. Their goal was to carry the torch of civilization to lesser peoples. Yet, sneered Régismanset, when the account books of overseas expansion were analyzed, it was the millions of francs in foreign trade that were counted, not the civilized souls.[36] What was forgotten was the fact that man is not civilized by being inflicted with moral theories and philosophical principles. What should alone be sought by the colonizing power is the increase of the native's physical wants and desires. But too many people, as a result of "hypocrisy or bad psychological analysis will read 'humanity,' that is, myth and abstraction, where one should read 'force,' that is, reality and substance." [37] In short, according to Régismanset's analysis, religion served to cover up man's actions.[38]

All colonial theories are dangerous, Régismanset concluded. They constitute dangerous generalizations "for they are the abstract and sterile forms of activity dressed in a rational figure." [39] Does not domination, pure and simple, suffice, he boldly asked? [40] On another occasion he had written that humanitarianism ought not to be brought forth as a motive when the real goal is one of conquest. The foolishness of assimilation is clear: one race cannot assimilate another; it only has two choices: subjugation or annihilation.[41]

Régismanset's sharp condemnation of French colonial theory and his insistence on force as the leitmotiv of overseas expansion were wide departures from the usual French interpretations. Proudly, Régismanset claimed he was the first in France to develop such a thesis. But he added that he was delighted that another person had taken up and expanded his argument.[42] This person was Jules Harmand.

Force and Domination: the Ideas of Jules Harmand

In his book, *Domination et colonisation*, one of the most important works on colonial theory published in France prior to the First World War, Harmand explained all colonial activity as the result of the natural instinct toward expansion.[43] His interpretation of this idea was but a repetition of the one widely fostered at the time: man, like all animals, seeks to expand in order to assure his self-preservation; human societies realize that in growing stronger and larger their chances of survival are better.[44] But for Harmand this instinct toward preservation was nothing more than Nietzsche's will to power.[45]

Convinced that such an instinct arises primarily from deeply felt anxiety, Harmand emphasized that this anxiety centers around two poles—need and fear—and is apparent wherever peoples intent upon seeking the necessary means of existence come into contact with one another. In primitive societies the will to power appears in all its simplicity and brutality, but in more advanced societies it is so well hidden by pretenses and elaborated motives that it is not initially seen. Whether expressed in terms of patriotism, courage, or the love of glory, the feeling remains basically one of fear. To alleviate this fear and to assure their continued existence all social organizations from the primitive family to the modern state seek to strengthen themselves with the purpose of checking or destroying their enemies.[46]

Until mankind finds some sort of lasting equilibrium, Harmand asserted, the expansion of nations can only be accomplished by means of continuous violence. Force alone will prevail. And it must be respected, Harmand added, for "it is a fatal obligation, an ineluctable necessity to which pitiless nature has subjected man. . . . it is necessary to recognize the fact that force itself is the basis of law." [47]

Up to this point Harmand had said nothing which really varied considerably with the ideas of Régismanset, and to this point he may have been indebted to Régismanset for his arguments, as the latter claimed. But thenceforth his ideas became far broader, expressing a variety of opinions held by other French imperialists and resulting from his own personal experience as well.

While he began his discussion of expansion with a brief analysis of what he called natural expansion, or that which was unorganized and without definite purpose,[48] Harmand dwelt more particularly on civilized, or politically directed, expansion,[49] a subject which led him to the problem of assimilation. In this matter Roman colonization offered an example which he believed had too long been neglected, for an analysis of Roman endeavors indicated the differences between ancient and modern expansion and also showed the fallacy of attempting assimilation in contemporary colonial activity.

The differences Harmand saw were chiefly of a geographical sort: modern colonialism occurs over vast distances; that of the ancient world was effected within contiguous regions.[50] To this thought he linked another: the ancient races coming into contact with other peoples were nowhere so widely separated culturally as are the modern races doing the same thing.

As the example of Gaul showed, Harmand continued, assimilation had been possible in earlier periods of colonization.[51] Not only did the Gauls appreciate and desire Roman culture and material progress, but they also viewed the *Pax Romana* as a boon, for it tended to diminish their internal squabbles and disorders. At first glance there might seem to be a similarity between the Roman occupation of Gaul and the British occupation of India; both assured public peace and welfare in a region rife with native warring factions. However, this comparison, cautioned Harmand, could be all too easily exaggerated. Above all the Europeans pertain to an entirely different civilization than that of their subject peoples so that the cultural gap separating conquered and conqueror cannot be bridged as it had been in the instance of Roman contiguous expansion.[52] Moreover, assimilation in Gaul only followed after social fusion between the peoples involved had taken place.[53] Where important differences did exist the Romans never attempted a policy of assimilation but rather employed a system comparable to that of the modern protectorate.[54] On this matter Harmand obviously differed with many of his fellow imperialists who were wont to consider French colonial theory synonymous with that of Rome.

The truly interesting reason for his repudiation of the doctrine of assimilation, however, did not pertain to cultural matters but rather stemmed from the earlier explanation of the role of force in all colonial expansion.

All conquests are immoral. This statement Harmand underlined.[55] To rob a people of its independence is an immoral act. Yet he believed that conquests are the results of imposed immorality, in turn the result of the universal law of the struggle for existence. One must conquer or die.[56] Evoking the often used argument of economic scarcity, Harmand insisted that vast regions of the world and the resources they contain could not be allowed to remain in a state of disuse because of the incompetence of their present occupants.

Here Harmand again agreed with Régismanset on the need for force in overseas expansion. As he saw it domination and force were correlatives.[57] Without force domination would be impossible.

Domination, a work of state, exerted on races too different from that of the conqueror to allow them to come into intimate contact with his race, presents an indelible foreign character. The two elements face-to-face are irreducible, or, as we say, unassimilable.[58]

The conqueror, generous as he might be, could never expect any real affection or sympathy from his subject peoples. Even after the lapse of a long period of time, when the two peoples would have both profited from the occupation, the conqueror would be foolish to believe that his domination had either become liked or accepted.[59] He had constantly to maintain his position by the sword. "This is the punishment for his violence, the stain of blood which nothing can eradicate from his hands." [60]

Then this sort of domination was incompatible with democracy. The result of force, it could only mean the creation of an aristocratic form of government in which there was no room for the principle of equality. The conquerer was left with no other choice than that of being the *bon tyran*, tolerant and charitable, but strong. Democratic institutions could not be brought into these regions of the world, for "subjects are not and cannot be citizens in the democratic sense of the word." [61]

Although few colonial theorists gave thought to the possible problems arising from the aggressive nature of modern imperialism as described by Régismanset and Harmand, mention was made on various occasions of this fundamental characteristic of imperialism. Jean de Lanessan, for instance, made the following statement:

The history of colonization is not only that of the migration of men across the world. It is also that of war and of the exploitation of races and nations by one another, the most intelligent and the strongest mercilessly abusing those which are less civilized and weaker.[62]

Even Chailley-Bert agreed with such a thought and, furthermore, seemed to follow Harmand's reasoning in his assertion that assimilation was untenable because the peoples subjected to French rule "do not welcome us and they do not love us as liberators; they hate us as conquerors." [63] Albert Sarraut's postwar interpretation of colonialism did not deviate much from these opinions. He considered colonial activity at its origin but an egotistical act of force, the justification of which was to be found in its utility, in the development and distribution of new wealth.[64]

The use of force and the assertion of the tenets of French colonial assimilation were thus considered incompatible in the starkly realistic world described by some colonial theorists. Not popular in a nation proud of its humanitarianism, these thoughts still lent weight to the arguments brought forth to explain the need for rejection of assimilation.

Chapter 6

A NEW POLICY: ASSOCIATION

ALTHOUGH denunciations of traditional French colonial policy and doctrine often appeared to be more ardent than attempts to substitute a new policy for the old, several new, if not original, plans for native administration did emerge at the beginning of the twentieth century. Essentially all resembled one another and were more often than not grouped together under the name of association.[1] Because of the almost generic sense in which it was used, the term, never sharply defined, was often fused with the idea of the colonial protectorate and was at times simply seized upon as a convenient catchword. Despite these shortcomings there was wide agreement on the general ideas which the term was to embrace.

The great virtue of this policy was proclaimed to lie in its simplicity, flexibility, and practicality. Opposed to the rigidity and universalism of the condemned doctrine of assimilation, the policy of association emphasized the need for variation in colonial practice. One of its essential tenets was the idea that the determining factors in all colonial policy should be the geographic and ethnic characteristics and the state of social development of the particular region submitted to foreign control. Evolution of native groups along their own lines was the key.

Underlying these thoughts was the realization that a strong type of cooperation between colonial and native was imperative. This would be best achieved, ran the accepted argument, through the retention of native institutions. All French efforts were to be directed toward developing the region; in this task French and natives would be "associated," each doing what best suited its abilities and stage of development.

Such a program necessitated a degree of autonomy in colonial administration unknown in France prior to the Third Republic. The doctrine of assimilation naturally implied centralization, and throughout her modern colonial history France had attempted to control colonial administration from Paris. Now, however, the demand for flexibility in actual practice made the former policy seem untenable. The block theory of colonialism was condemned. Not an empire, unified and homogeneous, but a series of unrelated possessions existed, and these demanded separate administration.[2] As a consequence the administrator-on-the-spot and the officials in his charge were to assume far more responsibility for the direction of the possession's affairs than heretofore, and the task of the minister of colonies, it was said, was to be limited solely to coordination of general colonial policy.[3] In short, the tradition of colonial assimilation was being discarded.

The idea of association was, of course, not entirely new, and even the use of the term, often credited first to Jules Harmand,[4] had an old history. René Maunier, in his work, *The Sociology of Colonies,* to which reference has already been made, traced the origin and growth of the idea. The type of association which he called "hierarchic partner-ship" [5] dovetailed with that discussed by the theorists at the beginning of the twentieth century. Maunier explained that colonial partnership went through three phases, phases which he considered in an ascendant order and in which first the idea and spirit of humanitarianism were expressed, then those of equality, and finally those of fraternity. It is in the first phase that association develops; here "there is no equality, but there is humanity and moderation. . . . there is collaboration and cooperation, but of superior and inferior." [6]

While inklings of this idea existed before the eighteenth century, it is at the end of that century that the idea be-came evident. In 1789 Robinet, in the *Dictionnaire universel des sciences morales*, expressed his desire for associa-tion between colonizer and native, and in 1821 the Comte de Laborde published his *L'Esprit d'association dans tous les intérêts de la communauté*, a work which discussed the colonial situation in Santo Domingo. Then Saint-Simon's chief disciple, Enfantin, described his own idealistic concept of association in the word *affamiliation*, which connoted intimate ties established between ruler and ruled. [7]

Germinated in the fertile soil of the Enlightenment, as were so many humanitarian ideas, and fed by the stream of thought emanating from the Quakers, [8] association then im-plied mutual trust and friendly cooperation, but of two differently developed peoples whose relationship was de-scribed as one of teacher—or of "governor" in the sense of preceptor [9]—and pupil. The idea was, perhaps, a variation

on the theme of the noble savage. And it is interesting to
note that the ideas of colonial association and of assimilation were largely inspired by common ideas. But whereas a
conscious lineal development in the instance of the doctrine
of assimilation can be easily traced, this cannot be done
for association. None of the colonial theorists were aware—
at least they made no indication that they were—of an
earlier use of the term "association" or of the idea as such.
One among them did state that the "formula is not new," [10]
but the others who interested themselves in the issue saw
the origin and growth of the term and idea as being com-
mensurate with the growth of an interest in native policy
and the concept of the colonial protectorate.

The native policy which France so sorely lacked, according to contemporary observers, was evolved in the
last few decades of the nineteenth century by several
colonial administrators, but most forcefully by two men
in particular: Gallieni and Lyautey. To understand more
fully the discussion of colonial theory in France, it is necessary to analyze briefly the methods of these two colonial
officers. To appreciate their methods, it is advisable to begin the story with a few words about their predecessor,
Faidherbe.

A Colonial Triumvirate: Faidherbe, Gallieni, Lyautey

Far from the effects of volatile public opinion and from
the interference of a Chamber of Deputies often hostile to
colonial undertakings, the new empire builders, best ex-

emplified by Faidherbe, Gallieni, and Lyautey, were able
to act as they saw fit. They were their own masters. Thus
they were able to analyze the colonial situation with a de-
tachment unknown in France and were able to pursue a
personal policy relatively unhindered by changing national
political pressures. On the scene, free from tradition and
historic polemics, they realized what many Frenchmen did
not: the essential difference between modern imperialism
and the earlier forms of French colonial activity.

France was not building another "New France." No
colonies de peuplement were necessary or desirable. With
her static population and her citizens' traditional love of
their native soil, France was spared the problem of search-
ing for outlets for emigration. Moreover, her newly acquired possessions were largely unsuited to white populations. Located in the tropics for the most part, these regions, with their profuse vegetation and hostile climate,
were not the sort to induce colonization. As many colonial
administrators clearly perceived, the true problem for
France was of an entirely different sort: the relationship
between a native mass and a white ruling minority. In the
second colonial empire this problem was relatively new.

The beginnings of a sound native policy can be traced
back to Dupleix in India or Montcalm in Canada. Nevertheless, it was not until a century later that the French
colonial administrators as a group became cognizant of the
virtues or even of the need of a native policy based on
mutual respect between themselves and the populations
they sought to rule. It could be said that they had no other

choice, and indeed their policy was expedient. But it was also humane: the outstanding French colonial figures of this period were men who loved the life they followed, approached the native populations in their charge with sympathy—of a condescending sort, perhaps—and devoted themselves to the welfare of these peoples almost as much as to the welfare of the state they served. There were scoundrels, it is true, but there were also people like Auguste Pavie. That remarkable Frenchman, who sought to be as much a part of the native life in Indochina as was possible, casts his shadow across the annals of French colonial history in the late nineteenth century. Pavie spoke of the *conquête des coeurs,* and his was really such a policy.[11] It was not limited to him, however.

The French Third Republic in the second and third decades of its existence produced a type of military officer who found in the pacification and administration of France's overseas possessions the opportunity to practice an art not suited to the European battlefield. Organization and administration were the activities in which he showed his skill, not in military strategy. In such endeavors Gallieni and Lyautey were the outstanding figures. Although they were two of the greatest administrators of colonial policy during the Third Republic, their methods followed in the tradition of native policy which had been encouraged by Léon Faidherbe.[12]

A professional soldier trained in colonial warfare and activities during his service with General Bugeaud in Algeria, Faidherbe developed his own methods in the Senegal where he first took up his duties in 1852 as officer in the corps of engineers. From this date, he devoted his life to the population of the Senegal and to the problems besetting it. So successful were his initial efforts that, upon the retirement of Governor Protet, the merchants of Saint Louis suggested Faidherbe as the likely candidate for the position. In 1854 he was appointed governor-general. Under his effective leadership the internecine wars between the various local native elements were soon checked, thus enabling the French to turn their full attention to matters of political organization and administration.

Imbued with traditional French principles of justice which led him to respect peoples of other races, Faidherbe struggled to improve the native's state while he subdued the region for France. It was his policy to use force only at the moment when peaceful methods did not bring the desired results. He assumed a position in opposition to many of the colonial administrators of his day, for he rejected the French love of abstract principles and taste for complicated bureaucracy; instead he followed a practical and simple program which was based on the needs of the local population and its environment. Wherever and to whatever extent possible he avoided any interference with the customs and habits of the local population. To his aides he solemnly declared: "The first requisite is to administer the conquered populations well. . . . Because of differences of race and religion, it is necessary to let them regulate their own affairs as much as possible." [13]

What Faidherbe was implementing in the Senegal was a

policy of penetration with the aid of the native populations. Thus he sought to maintain whatever effective native institutions he found to be of advantage. When Gallieni arrived in the Senegal, he saw before him the excellent results of Faidherbe's native policy.

Ardent republican, a man of thought and of action, endowed with acute intelligence, Gallieni left France in 1877 for the Senegal where his vocation of colonizer opened before him. "I love this life," he said, and he applied himself to colonial problems with the same enthusiasm that characterized Faidherbe. Although ten years after his arrival there he was named commandant of the French Sudan, his real talents became manifested more clearly in Tonkin.

When Gallieni arrived in Tonkin in 1892, the French colonial government there was shaken by the struggles and piracy carried on by Chinese bands in spite of the fact that France had earlier made peace with China. Under the initiative of Governor-General Lanessan, an able administrator who also contributed to French colonial theory, the Upper Tonkin, where these struggles were most evident, was divided into four military districts. One of these territories was confided to Gallieni. His lightning-like achievements led Lanessan to give him the most troubled region, that which centered around Langson. Gallieni ended the pirate problem by a careful application of his own colonial policy:

To occupy the country firmly, to win over the natives and to make them participate in the effort we are undertaking, such were essentially the principles to be applied in order to save the Upper Tonkin from the anarchy from which it suffered.[14]

Gallieni's method was simple, a combination of good sense and basic psychology. To protect the country against further pirate attacks, he had a chain of military posts constructed. These were made of concrete to convince the local natives of the French intention to stay and thus to rally them to the French side. He took the "inhabitants of the country as chief collaborators" against his enemies, and he employed them as often as possible in the local administration of the region.[15]

This policy, first undertaken in Tonkin, reached its final form at Madagascar, where Gallieni gained his greatest reputation. In no region were the French more confused or insecure than on this island, the occupation of which had begun during the second ministry of Jules Ferry. Anarchy still reigned, stimulated by continual insurrection and assisted by the lack of experience among the French in charge of the occupation. These were the reasons for which Gallieni was called to Madagascar in 1896. Immediately charged with the task of pacifying the island, he destroyed the Hova Kingdom, which occupied the central plateau of the island. Then he liberated the other native peoples formerly under Hova control, confiding the region of the extreme south to Lyautey. With speed that amazed the French government Gallieni subdued all of Madagascar and, in 1905, when he left and retired from colonial life, the island was peaceful and on the way to prosperity.

It was during his mission to Madagascar that Gallieni perfected his colonial policy. The best explanations of this policy are to be found in the proclamations that he wrote at the time.

Gallieni's method was founded on the immediate, the necessary, and the opinion that: "the administrative organization of a new country must be in perfect rapport with its resources, its geographic configurations, the mentality of its inhabitants, and the goal that one proposes to attain." [16] In his instructions of May 22, 1898, on the pacification of Madagascar he declared that the best means of attaining this goal was to employ the combined action of force and politics.[17] This he explained in two expressions which soon became famous: *la tache d'huile* and the *politique des races*.

According to Gallieni it was best to use force in a limited way only. Immediately after the pacification of some territory, permanent posts, political centers, and means of communication were to be established. Then the advance would continue slowly; the region would be cleared of the enemy with the help of the local inhabitants now won over to the French cause and duly armed for their new task. Provisional posts would be established in the newly acquired regions, and the process would thus continue until the whole region had been conquered and pacified. "This is the method of the *tache d'huile*. New territory is not acquired until all that in the rear had been completely organized." [18]

If force was needed as a means of assuring colonial control, political action was still more important. A knowledge of the country and of its inhabitants was imperative, for upon these elements depended the type of government which would be instituted and, consequently, the very success of this government. Gallieni believed that not only were there customs which had to be respected but also there were hates and rivalries among the peoples which could be exploited.[19] Like every clever and able leader, he knew the value of the old adage, *divide et impera*.

Following this empirical program Gallieni pacified Madagascar. In the process he developed the second of his famous principles, the *politique des races*. As a general rule he assumed that "all administrative organization must follow the country in its natural development." [20] The native bureaucracy was to be left intact wherever possible; administration was to be flexible and based on the needs of each region; and, finally, all reforms were to be carefully studied in terms of native needs so as to avoid the disastrous results obtained in colonies where European institutions had been introduced *en bloc*.[21] This *politique des races* was progressive in nature and based upon means as well as ends. As Gallieni himself wrote:

Nothing is more damaging . . . in colonial affairs than preconceived formulas, imported principles, which, based most often on European ideas, do not apply to the environments, situations, or occasions for which one has wanted to adapt them. Common sense, knowledge of the country and of its inhabitants, prudent initiative directed toward the general goal desired, these must be the principal guides of our civilian and military administrators.[22]

Nothing could be farther from the traditional doctrine of assimilation. No method seemed more attractive to the colonial officers who were then winning new regions for the

French empire.[23] Among these officers, one incorporated Gallieni's ideas with his own, proved their worth, and won himself a name as a genius in colonial affairs. This was Lyautey.

Gallieni had no disciple more devoted than Hubert Lyautey, even though their personal backgrounds contrasted markedly. A member of a well-known monarchist family which had produced good soldiers for monarchy and empire alike,[24] Lyautey served the Third Republic well. If Gallieni had simple tastes and prided himself on his republican sentiments, Lyautey remained a traditionalist and a lover of the refined way of life. Yet both men possessed a humanitarian spirit. In the service of Gallieni in Tonkin, Lyautey found his reason for being: he was seduced by colonial life. He admired Gallieni as man and administrator, and he hastened to adopt Gallieni's methods.[25]

The close friendship between the two men developed in Tonkin, where Gallieni asked for and received Lyautey as his chief of staff. From this period, Lyautey's devotion for his chief continued to grow. The novice soon acquired experience and won the admiration of his senior, who took him with him when he was given the task of pacifying Madagascar.

At Madagascar Lyautey's abilities were soon recognized and, in 1900, Gallieni entrusted the high command of the south, a heavy responsibility at the time, to Lyautey. Lyautey's own development of a native policy can be dated from this period. It is the policy of Gallieni with greater emphasis placed on the idea of the protectorate. After van-

quishing the rebel chief, Rabezavena, and then winning him
over to the French side, Lyautey exclaimed, *"Vive la
méthode Gallieni!* Here again it has proved itself; it certainly is the true colonial method." [26] During the entire cam-
paign in the south Lyautey applied Gallieni's techniques with
success, and, when the region was completely pacified, he
defined his version of the policy in the following words:

To adopt the policy and administration of the protectorate sig-
nifies: to maintain as much as possible in their entirety native
governmental machinery, institutions, and customs; to use the
traditional leaders, to let them control the police, the administration—even justice—and the collection of taxes, under the simple control of a single agent residing close to the chief.[27]

What was here suggested was to be the basis of the administrative policy which was applied with success in
Morocco. In fact, Lyautey's elaboration of the protectorate
regime, his respect for Moslem customs, and his retention of
the old Cherifian government—if only as a façade—proved so
efficacious that, at the beginning of the First World War, he
could proudly send the better part of his French troops to
Europe.

In 1924, at the termination of his remarkable career in
Morocco, Lyautey lauded the method developed by Gallieni
and perfected by himself, when, in a speech at Casablanca,
he declared:

This agreeable and candid association of the two races is the
best and surest guarantee of the future in Morocco. Nothing
durable is based on force. The intelligent and hard-working
people we have found here have quickly realized all the material benefits we have brought them as well as the assurance of

peace and order, business security, and economic equipment we have brought. But that which has brought us still more good will is the fact that we have shown our esteem for this people by having respected all they respect, by assuring them the retention of their traditional institutions. In a word we have placed our hand in theirs.[28]

Although the colonial officers here briefly mentioned were among the best known of those who asserted a new colonial policy, they were not alone. For instance, General Pennequin, who had originally served under Pavie in Indochina, acquired two admirers in Gallieni and Lyautey by his practice of a sound native policy and the use of indigenous troops in the conquest of the area around the Red River in 1892.[29] Pennequin's superior, governor-general Jean-L. de Lanessan (1891–94), was one of the first to see the need for a well-followed policy of association. Seeking to avoid the heavy administrative machinery with which the French often weighted their colonies, he envisaged a form of indirect rule which would utilize existing native elites by associating them with the French effort. He suggested that the French leave local administration in the hands of the Annamite officials, "whom we will guide by our counsels and surround with our control." [30]

While Indochina remained the experimental grounds for a new and vigorous colonial policy pushed by a small group of resolved men, even in the depths of Africa, where the native problem might seem to be of a different order, the need for cooperation was asserted. Savorgnan de Brazza wrote in his *Correspondances:* "To make use of the natives, to identify their interest and ours, to make them our natural allies, this was one of the most important aims of my mission in my opinion." [31]

If the ideas and practices of these men had been adumbrated by others before them, the growing range of agreement is of considerable importance. At home the theorists and popularizers were engaged in giving verbal expression to the body of knowledge which the colonial administrators were using. This was a time when the methods already followed in the overseas regions profoundly influenced the theories in France. Practice seemed to be preceding theory.

Explanation of the Policy of Association

The ideas generally included in the policy of association for the most part mirrored the methods practiced by Gallieni and Lyautey. The true significance of "association" is found in the belief that the economic betterment of the region was to be undertaken by native and Frenchman within the general framework of native institutions. It was a policy based on the acceptance of mutual interests and on a sort of fraternity, but not of equality.

No more interesting an explanation of the policy of association is to be found than that given by Jules Harmand in his *Domination et colonisation*. For Harmand, association was synonymous with cooperation, a policy by which the conqueror would be most able to develop the conquered region economically, but also one in which the conqueror realized his responsibility to the native and concerned himself with that person's mental and physical well-being. While he believed association could be applied almost anywhere as an economic principle or moral guide, Harmand insisted that as a political instrument association would be most satisfactory where a homogeneous and relatively civilized population was to be found, and where, as he frankly admitted, submission to foreign control would be most difficult to achieve.[32]

As with all advocates of association, Harmand listed among the policy's salient features tolerance, respect for native customs and laws, cooperation and assistance in place of exploitation. The base upon which Harmand's idea of association was to be established was order.[33] According to him the chief factor lacking in the more advanced native societies was stable, orderly government. Afflicted by a shortage of capital, a lack of scientific know-how, by external threats and internal corruption, the native governments found it impossible to emerge from their sad state. A foreign government both strong and efficient could do what the native government could not in assuring peace and prosperity. And it seems that in offering this argument Harmand sought to justify the act of force which he insisted imperialism was.

The most novel idea that Harmand had to offer was one which seemed to be inferred in the policy of association but which was first clearly stated by him: association involved a sort of contractual agreement. It was a contract which "envisages the coexistence and cooperation of two profoundly different societies placed in contact in a manner as brusque as it is artificial." [34] In practice the arrangement would give the European responsibility to produce material benefits valuable to native civilization. For his part, the native, gradually reflecting on the values derived from his forced subordination, would begin to cooperate more fully with the European. In short, the policy was, in Harmand's opinion, the "systematic repudiation of assimilation," for it encouraged the retention of native institutions and implied a large degree of administrative autonomy. [35]

Although Harmand praised the policy of association as the best of all available colonial policies for control of native populations, he did caution about a possible danger in its application. The acknowledged French tendency in colonial administration might easily lead to "excessive liberalism." [36] While the idea of a contract did exist, this contract implied no equality among the participants, Harmand affirmed. The occupying power had to retain its primacy.

> The policy of association, realistic and intelligent, reserves with unshakable firmness all rights of domination and takes into account all its exigencies. It does not at all attempt to prepare and achieve an equality forever impossible, but rather it attempts to establish a certain equivalence or compensation of reciprocal services. Far from letting the domination weaken, this policy wants to reinforce it by making it less offensive and repugnant. [37]

In no way, however, did the newly proposed policy of association as explained by Harmand and others completely repudiate France's traditional *mission civilisatrice;* it merely modified it. In the first place the occupation of a colonial region still implied a moral obligation which was to be fulfilled by the improvement of the native's material and cultural status. However, rather than repeat the errors of assimilation by attempting to utilize methods little in accord with local customs, the French were gradually to introduce institutions and benefits which would be advantageous to the natives and appreciated by them.[38] In the second place, so that their economic goals would be reached, the French would be compelled to impose certain French institutions on the inhabitants of the subdued region. Nevertheless, these too were to be introduced, wherever necessary, within the frame work of native society. Thus, in theory the policy of association differed from that of assimilation in that the former sought the improvement of the native's condition without severely altering his way of life, while the latter sought the reorganization of native society in the light of French civilization.

To the ardent adherents of the new theory practical application appeared easy, provided certain necessary conditions existed. First, respect between Frenchman and native had to be assured so that rapid cooperation between the two would ensue. Second, realization of the responsibility of the one group to the other for the betterment of the region was necessary. Third, a sufficiently developed native administration was indispensable if the natives were to govern themselves adequately so that economic cooperation and development could take place under peaceful, even harmonious, conditions. For this last reason association was usually considered most feasible for Indochina.[39]

Although Jules Harmand was the theorist credited with first advancing the policy of association as such, it was the Minister of Colonies, Clémentel, who may be considered the first to give this policy official sanction and to forward it.[40] In 1905, speaking on several occasions to the ardent supporters of French imperialism, he signaled the need of a native policy which made the native an associate of the Frenchman in his task of improving the colonial region. "This policy of collaboration, of association is, moreover, a necessary policy. It constitutes not only a policy of justice but also a policy of foresight and of security." [41]

Clémentel did not limit himself to words but sought to put such a policy into effect. In December, 1905, he inaugurated his colonial program with two letters of instruction to the governors of Indochina and Madagascar. Of Indochina he wrote that its betterment had to be achieved through "the protection, education, and association of the native." [42] These were also the means by which he hoped to gain the confidence and support of the native populations: "Participating directly in all the efforts of this nature, reassured by employment of men of their own race, they [the populations] will soon realize that the goal sought is neither contrary to their customs nor beyond their capacities." [43] As for Madagascar, Clémentel wished to continue Gallieni's policies there. The native bureaucrats were to be increased in number and associated in the work carried on by the French in the various provinces. In addition, greater local administrative autonomy was to be granted.[44]

Clémentel tried to introduce this new colonial policy at the same time that the colonial congresses were urging the policy themselves. These congresses, of importance because they brought together the "colonial party," were the scenes of many discussions of colonial theory. Although this particular problem received no more treatment than any other, the various publications of proceedings indicate that warm approval was given to the policy of association. At the French Colonial Congress of 1905 Joseph Caillaux insisted that "our policy must gradually be a policy of association." [45] Again in 1906, at the large Colonial Congress of Marseilles, the policy of association was acclaimed. [46] Finally, in 1907, at the annual French Colonial Congress, it was said with confidence: "The entire colonial group is in agreement on the necessity of following this policy of association." [47] Paul Deschanel added that the doctrine of assimilation had seen its day, and "we are today about to apply this formula of association which the colonial congresses have already determined and illuminated." [48]

This brief indication of the ideas expressed during the colonial congresses—in large measure the barometer of the imperialist faction in France—shows that the policy of association was now being accepted. Nevertheless, extensive studies or explanations of this policy were not to be found. By its very nature association had to be vague; it was a general policy, not a detailed program. And it was as much a solution to France's colonial problems as would be any colonial policy short of withdrawal.

Like the doctrine of assimilation before it, association was willingly accepted; it appeared to be a practical and simple idea which sold itself without the need of extensive advertising.

Association and the Protectorate

The relationship between the idea of association and that of the colonial protectorate resulted in some confusion in the period under study, as it has in subsequent analyses of that period.[49] The fact that both ideas were without precise definition and hence subject to wide usage, that both were rather contemporaneous in formulation, and that both were usually suggested for application in the same overseas regions only compounded the confusion.

Actually some of the colonial theorists of the period declared association to be nothing more than a new name for the protectorate. Wrote Chailley-Bert: "Everyday the newspapers fling about the idea of association of whites and natives. The word 'association' is perhaps a new word, but those persons who are my age and who took part in the former struggle can say that it is we who are the real authors of this policy; it was formerly called the protectorate." [50]

The application of the protectorate to colonial problems was relatively new in France. Although a rudimentary form of this regime had already appeared in Tahiti as early as the July Monarchy, it was with the acquisition of Tunisia that the protectorate became clearly established and

thoroughly appreciated. Jules Ferry was therefore correct
in calling it a new system of administration.[51]

According to Pierre Lyautey the Tunisian protectorate
issued from a conversation held between Gabriel Hanotaux and Jules Ferry just before the signing of the Treaty
of Bardo.[52] Hanotaux, in the role of historian, recalled the
advantages derived from a protectorate system at the time
of the Treaty of Cateau-Cambrésis, when the three
bishoprics of Toul, Metz, and Verdun were submitted to
such a regime. Ferry was so taken with the idea that it
served as inspiration in his instructions to the first French
resident-general.

The immediate source of the idea is less important than
the results which were derived from its political realization.
The success of the Tunisian venture went far in convincing the French that the protectorate idea was a sound one.
Initially the status of Tunisia remained vague under the
Treaty of Kassar-Said and was not really defined until the
Treaty of Marsa mentioned the word protectorate. During
the interval France's political attitude was summed up nega-
tively in the phrase, "neither annexation nor abandon-
ment." [53] Outright annexation did not suit France's policy
at the time; [54] thus Hanotaux's solution was a happy one,
and one which the administration of Paul Cambon made
successfully function.

Cambon, as first resident-general, established an effective
and practical relationship between the French and the
Tunisians which enabled the beylic government to retain
its outward signs of power and authority. He sought to

make few changes and desired to retain a simple administration. Of his results Cambon wrote: "Thanks to this system we were more the master of the populations here in four years than in Algeria after fifty-five years of conquest." [55]

Soon the practice inspired the theory, and analyses of the protectorate in matters of international law and internal administration began to appear. Chailley-Bert was able to write: "The word 'protectorate' is but a label which conveniently allows the most varied combinations, often even the most conflicting." [56] And Hanotaux himself once commented that the idea of the protectorate evaded definition and was nothing more than a "statement of fact." [57] In view of such comments it should not be surprising that a variety of protectorate relationships emerged in theory,[58] some of which were identical to the policy of association.

If the use of the term "protectorate" only became widespread during the period of modern imperialism, the practice was old, as contemporary Frenchmen were wont to demonstrate.[59] The Greeks and Romans had utilized such regimes, realizing the advantages that could be provided by them. In a more recent period Bodin discussed the concept of protection and how it could function effectively.[60] Perhaps these older ideas of the protectorate differed from the colonial one, as some Frenchmen believed.[61] The older concept was considered to imply a relationship between two states, one stronger than the other, but both of a similar degree of civilization. What the stronger one did was provide his protection, receiving in return tribute, or military aid if necessary. The new idea of the colonial protectorate implied a relationship between two peoples of unequal development, and the idea of tutelage consequently ensued.

In terms of practicality the colonial protectorate provided a convenient and relatively inexpensive means by which the French could control the area they had subdued. At times this was considered a temporary arrangement, perhaps, but a step toward annexation and absorption. In the opinion of one French critic, who compared the policy of annexation with that of the protectorate, the protectorate was but an administrative form: "Annexation is the genus; the protectorate is the species." [62] Another author believed that occupation of a territory under the title of protectorate was the initial means by which to gain control of that territory's sovereignty.[63]

On the level of international affairs the protectorate admirably suited the French imperialists' needs and objectives. Chiefly, it removed any number of international problems bound to arise as a result of direct annexation. In theory the protected state was still sovereign, although direction of its foreign affairs was one of the chief demands of the protecting power.[64] Another claimed advantage was the loose control which Paris and its bureaucrats would have over the protected area. Certainly the resident-general would have considerable autonomy in internal matters and might well be able to obviate some of the more blatant abuses stemming from excessive centralization.

In its general characteristics the idea of the protectorate

appeared to resemble, if not to parallel, the idea of association. The decentralization, the respect for native institutions and control through them, the flexibility contained within the one idea were found within the other as well. So was the expected economy of operation.

Particularly when considered as an internal policy, a system for governing native populations, the protectorate seemed at one with the policy of association in the thoughts of some contemporary Frenchmen. Jules Ferry's conception of the protectorate is an example at hand. The function of the protectorate, Ferry wrote, was reform from above, slowly wrought by means of existing native administration. Avoiding the absolutes of former colonial policy, the protectorate regime best reflected the flexibility needed. It accommodated itself to various colonial situations facing France by working with the native elite in the existing native framework.[65] Albert Vignon, an able thinker enlisted in the colonial cause, defined the protectorate tersely as "the science of administering the natives by intermediary of their natural leaders." [66] A similar definition, but with a different twist, was given after the First World War: "Politically, association finds its best form in the system of the protectorate which leaves the natives the grand avenues of power but places European administrators at strategic intersections." [67]

The easiest way to avoid the confusion that can ensue from a reading of the opinions and interpretations of contemporary French theorists on both the protectorate regime and the policy of association is to realize that the two policies were not necessarily connected. Association was an answer to the native problem. Its purpose, in the well-known words of Waldeck-Rousseau, was "to develop the natives in the framework of their own civilization." [68] Its purpose was also more mundane—economic cooperation. But association was restricted to internal matters, and it could function in areas not submitted to the regime of the protectorate. This was suggested by some writers. [69]

The protectorate idea was primarily an administrative one on an international level. As expedient as it was practical, it provided a solution to the problem of the relationship to be established between France and her overseas possessions. As *colonies de peuplement* were not needed, there was no imperative need for direct annexation. Indeed, the protectorate may be considered, as it has been, the regime which best complements the ideas of Jules Ferry on the economic need for expansion. [70] As outlets for French goods and capital were supposedly needed, regions controlled by France through a protectorate would provide this and would be inexpensive to manage.

The idea of the protectorate and that of association did overlap in the thoughts of French writers. In terms of development, the protectorate is older. But association was called forth on several occasions to be the policy which could help make the protectorate work and prosper. In 1912 the resident-general of Tunisia, Alapetite, stated: "France can do nothing serious or lasting in Africa without a close and cordial cooperation with the native populations submitted to our protection." [71] Similar statements were made about Indochina. But perhaps Lyautey best expressed the idea when he stated with reference to Morocco: "We are here in a protectorate where nothing can be achieved without cooperation. And cooperation requires that there be two parties." [72]

Even with its hazy lines of definition and interpretation the policy of association was of considerable importance in that it helped destroy the traditional basis of French colonial doctrine.[73] Until some time after the First World War the policy of association was widely regarded with favor. Its partisans insisted that it was efficacious because it was scientifically sound, practical, and above all, economical. In short, association appeared to be the solution to the perplexing native problem in modern French colonialism.

Chapter 7

ECONOMIC NEEDS AND THE
POLICY OF ASSOCIATION

THE very nature of the French colonial empire explains in large measure the development of the policy of association at the turn of the century. Spread widely over the globe and scarcely favorable to French immigration,[1] the empire depended entirely on the close cooperation of the native populations for its success. Colonial theorists and popularizers, convinced that the doctrine of assimilation would hinder rather than help colonial development, encouraged the new interest in a sound native policy. They were insistent that the realization of such a policy would assure the immediate cooperation of the native, henceforth deemed necessary to resolve the basic problems resulting from the avowed economic necessity of overseas expansion.

The essential point affirmed was the requirement of native labor for the economic development of the possessions. For, once economically bettered, the possessions were to be a source of markets for French manufactured goods and a source of raw materials. Such was the assertion of most of the imperialists who lived in an age when the most common justification for overseas expansion was one based on economic needs.[2]

"France will be colonial or she will not be." [3] This maxim was variously expressed in both economic and political terms. Leroy-Beaulieu interpreted it nationalistically when he proclaimed: "Colonization is for France a question of life or death." [4] Henri Mager spoke of it economically: "Without colonies, no more exportation." [5] And Jules Ferry, in a famous phrase, warned of France's economic plight thusly: "The protectionist system is a steam engine without a safety valve if it does not have as a corrective and auxiliary a sane and sound colonial policy." [6]

All of these opinions and countless more like them were fostered at the end of the nineteenth century at a time during which the economic situation of Europe appeared very somber. The economic crises of 1882 and 1890 shook European economies and frightened the most intrepid businessmen. The policy of protectionism—now followed nearly everywhere in Europe—and the rapid industrialization of the United States and Germany appeared to menace Europe with a lack of markets on one hand and overproduction on the other. Such problems greatly concerned France, herself not that far beyond the periphery of modern industrialization. For their part French imperialists were cognizant of these concerns and signaled that the colonies would serve as the needed outlets for metropolitan goods. They considered imperialism largely from the economic point of view. [7]

But France did not construct a new colonial empire primarily for economic reasons. The now famous Hobson-

Lenin analysis of the close relationship between the capitalist economy and overseas expansion fits uncomfortably into the history of France here under consideration.[8] The French economy as it existed at the end of the nineteenth century could hardly be called expansive, and the French capitalist was more a cautious investor than an adventuresome speculator. French industry produced slowly for a Western-refined and relatively wealthy clientele. Moreover, as had often been pointed out, the French banker followed the caprices of his heart or the shrewdness of his mind, not strictly national purpose; money flowed in Europe and even in Latin America with much stronger current than it did in the colonies.[9]

The long and short of it is the French did not see in their colonies lucrative markets and fertile fields for investment. Recent explanations of this are not infrequent. M. Raymond Aron has insisted that the building of the second colonial empire was not the work of French business because it was not dynamic enough;[10] another French author has stated that the French bourgeoisie was not imaginative enough to have helped precipitate the overseas ventures.[11] And, perhaps, as some Frenchmen affirm, the ill effects of the John Law financial debacle and the Panama Canal scandal somewhat tempered the French investor. Whatever the reasons, the economic argument for colonial expansion was neither presented by the world of French business nor greatly heeded by it.

In truth, the partisans of imperialism, for the most part

strong nationalists and republicans satisfied with the existing domestic regime,[12] sought to enlist support for their
cause by using the appeal of the economic argument. In
place of Jules Ferry stood a new herald of economic imperialism, Eugène Etienne. Affectionately called "our
chief" by the members of the colonial party, he exercised a
considerable influence on colonial affairs, not only in his
capacity as deputy and *colon* from Algeria but even more
as acknowledged guiding light of the amorphous colonial
group in the Chamber of Deputies.

His contribution to the colonial cause was not one of
originality but rather one of popularization. He devoted
his talents to the task of convincing the French parlia-
mentarians of the value of France's overseas empire. Probably because he acknowledged himself the heir to Ferry's
colonial efforts, he echoed the opinions Ferry held on the
economic importance of the colonies.

Etienne's colonial policy might easily be summed up by
the word "utility." As he himself declared: "It appears
clear that the sole criterion to apply to every colonial enterprise is its degree of utility, the sum of advantages and
profits flowing from it to the *métropole*." [13]

Chief in his mind was concern over the need for colonial
markets. He envisioned the disadvantages resulting from
new economic competition, particularly that from the
United States, and once rhetorically asked his fellow
deputies in the Chamber of Deputies what France would do
with her products if she could no longer export them.[14]

His own answer to such a question was found in his belief that the colonies would constantly provide a sure and exclusive market for French overproduction. Without mincing words he affirmed that the essential reason for the establishment of the French colonial empire was "the belief, the hope that the French industrialist and the French merchant would be able to dump their excess production in the colonies." [15]

Etienne was not, however, advocating a return to the old *Pacte coloniale*. He believed in the need to better native society, to introduce many of the benefits derived from French civilization. But he also did not wander from his utilitarian approach to the problem. He was determined that the colonies should remain markets. For this reason he thought the colonies should be confined to supplying necessary raw materials to France and to raising agricultural products not available at home.[16] What Etienne most ardently desired to avoid was economic competition between colony and mother country. What he wished the French to do was to consider their colonial problems from the position of businessmen and to administer the colonies in the manner of good merchants.[17] Yet these ideas were not restricted to Etienne; they were expressed in all French colonial circles.

At the beginning of the twentieth century French colonial policy could have been summarized in one sentence: "Every colonial enterprise is a business which must be prudently and practically conducted." [18] French the-

orists sought those colonial methods which would most
readily lead to the attainment of the prescribed economic
goal.

The Movement Toward "Association"

For a long time French imperialists had written their
opinions on the best means by which to make France's
colonial endeavors pay. Much had been said about the
need for trained personnel—a need now partly filled
through the work of the *Ecole coloniale*—and, above all,
the need for large sums of capital.[19] The native most often
figured in the background of the picture: he was considered the source of physical power by which the
colonist's brain and money would be profitably employed.

A large part of the discussion aroused during the dispute
over policy and doctrine resulted from a new evaluation of
the position of the native. If the native was still to supply
the needed muscle, he was also to be given a more pleasant
life than heretofore by his conquerors who, in turn, were to
assure him the maintenance of his institutions, a reasonable
share of the material benefits derived from the development
of the land, and a certain control of local administration.
This was the hope of contemporary imperialists; it was also
the core of the policy of association as seen from an economic point of view.

Already in 1897 Jean de Lanessan had indicated the
trend of this thought in his book *Principes de colonisation.*

His avowed purpose for writing this book was to study the principles upon which future colonial policy was to be based.[20] His study led him to advocate the protectorate as the soundest possible colonial system for those regions sufficiently advanced to receive it. Although Lanessan did not employ the term "association" in this particular analysis, he later related the term to the protectorate idea by asserting that "association" was only a new name for it.[21]

A sound native policy was essential, Lanessan believed, to assure the prosperity of the colonies and in order to win the support of the populations upon whom this prosperity depended. The less interference with local customs, the less obstacles to be encountered by the French and hence the more rapid the development of the region.[22] Therefore, it was necessary to protect the native from the European tendency toward outward exploitation and also to see that the native's religion and customs were respected. In short, the French were to make every race an "object of toleration." [23]

The program that Lanessan proposed in order to fulfill these requirements was of two sorts, depending on whether the colony had an effective overall native government or only possessed effective administration on the local level.[24] In the first instance Lanessan recommended a protectorate of a liberal sort; in the second, control of local affairs was to be given to native authorities to the extent that they were able to govern effectively. Every colony was thus to have a comparatively large degree of control over its own administration, and this administration itself was to retain as much of its original character as possible.

What Lanessan really sought was a type of administration kept as simple as possible and costing as little as possible. He emphasized that "the political and administrative organization of the colonies must be inspired by the thought of making their development as quick as possible, for the quicker they progress the sooner the *métropole* will be able to obtain profits from them." [25]

On the whole, Lanessan's ideas were paralleled by those of Auguste Billiard that were explained in *Politiques et organisations coloniales*, published in 1899. In agreement with Etienne, Billiard declared that French colonial policy was pursued as a direct outcome of industrial overproduction.[26] The colonies were to be privileged markets for France; to arrive at this state the administration which would most effectively encourage the native consumption of French products was to be fostered. According to Billiard, the primary problem facing the French was the improvement of the native economy so that the natives would be in a position to afford French products.[27] Hence there was a need for effective cooperation between the colonist and the native. Billiard envisoned this in the old formula: the colonist represented "the intelligent direction" in the possession; the native, the "brute force." [28]

Billiard definitely cast aside the doctrine of assimilation. He believed that because the mores of a people are "the natural fruit of the local environment and of atavistic legacies," [29] there is no question of substituting foreign mores for them. If attempted, the introduction of foreign ideas would only stimulate long and costly internecine struggles because of continuous native opposition to this aspect of foreign rule. Therefore, a policy of assimilation would signify nothing less than a period of trouble which would retard the economic development of the colony and ultimately lead to the mother country's loss of her privileged position in the region. An autonomous regime which would "involve the least change in the appearance of things" would be the best.[30]

The protectorate best met the above mentioned needs, according to Billiard. By taking the protected state *en bloc*, including all of its institutions, the protectorate would prove the most economical governmental system for the French and thus the most desirable.[31] Nevertheless, where the necessary conditions for establishing a protectorate did not exist,[32] direct administration, yet with respect for native institutions, would guarantee the best results.[33]

The only reproach that might be made against autonomy, Billiard believed, was that of the future possibility of the colony's political independence. A needless thought, he felt. That every human association reaches the point where its component elements have a tendency to break away could not be doubted. This is the case with the family; it is also the case with colonies.[34] Instead of trying to "eternalize" colonial relationships, the French would be pursuing a far sounder policy if they sought to find the best means by which to guarantee temporary subordination.

Neither force nor affection would suffice. The only sound alternative was an alliance in which each ally "finds a sufficient proportion of advantages so that he is willing to accept frankly the correlative inconveniences." [35]

As a matter of fact Billiard's proposals were quite simple: "That which it behooves us to introduce into our colonies are neither philosophical theories nor social institutions of a contingent value, but simply our manufactured products." [36]

At the Colonial Congress of 1904 similar ideas were again expressed. Following the advice of Eugène Etienne, who counseled the Congress to be practical,[37] its delegates declared themselves in favor of a program of cooperation between colonist and native. The resolution made by the First Section of the Congress (General Organization of the Colonies) discarded the old assimilative idea. Considering dangerous any attempt at assimilation of races by the sole means of education, and declaring that the "fusion of interests through economic development" was the best means by which to better the condition of the natives, the Congress resolved that "colonial governments concentrate their efforts on the economic development most likely to assure their well-being along with that of the colonists." [38]

In his report to the Congress Albert de Pouvourville went further.[39] As the natives were the source of manpower, he wrote, they must be utilized—associated with the economic task at hand. Therefore the problem to be solved was essentially one of making the native understand the need to work, to inculcate in him the notion that work is not only a right but an obligation. The *coloniaux de doctrine*—those who advocated assimilation—sought "absolute liberty for the natives, reaching the point of license." [40] The *coloniaux d'affaires*—those who knew the colonies—wanted a "reasonable constraint by work" [41] because, continued Pouvourville, work is one of the best means by which to civilize native populations. When the native works he brings benefits to his community and to the "protector" who aspires to increase the prosperity of the native's region. As a result, "the protector and the protected will gain equal advantages by coming to agreement in order that the region now jointly held will become fruitful." [42]

Outside of the Congress this theory was explained in clear terms by Georges Valmor in his *Les Problèmes de la colonisation*. Outlining the task facing France after the immediate problem of military conquest was over, he laid particular stress on the economic aspect, while clearly seeing the need for good political organization.[43] Important, after the natives had been pacified, was the return of native land and the encouragement of native labor. Equally important was the beginning of public works designed to facilitate the economic betterment of the region.[44]

With an eye open to the various problems involved in these undertakings, Valmor discussed the question of native labor. He believed that, if necessary, even forced labor was permissible, particularly in those regions without sufficient means of transportation and communication. Further, he believed such a policy would be justified in that the native himself would eventually profit from it through the economic prosperity of the region.[45]

However, the indifference or distaste manifested by native populations toward work of any kind hindered these operations, Valmor remarked.[46] The conqueror, therefore, had the pressing duty of accustoming the native to work. Valmor denounced assimilation because European institutions were too highly developed for the native and, moreover, gave him the impression he might do as he pleased.

The civilized person has the task of facilitating the evolution of the primitive through work and the task of elevating him to the heights of a man conscious of his obligations and of his dignity, rather than abandoning him to his base inclinations by a sort of stupid and sterile philanthropy.[47]

Granted that this argument was far from the vaunted French attitude toward native populations, it did emphasize the thoroughly practical nature of the new policy advocated by the imperialists in France. Valmor was stressing the point that all the resources of the colony, human and material, should be brought together to assure one concerted and effective economic effort. This was his interpretation of the policy of association.[48]

Essentially the policy of association which Jules Harmand upheld had economic roots also. Believing that France of necessity had to possess an overseas empire as a condition of national freedom and greatness, he did not want to see this empire prove to be a financial burden. On the contrary, he hoped the empire would be self-supporting.

What France had to do was to find the surest method by which to obtain from the empire "the maximum of advantages for the minimum of inconveniences." [49] To meet this objective Harmand proposed a policy which he considered utilitarian. He agreed with the Encyclopedists that the "colonies were made by and for the mother country." Yet he asserted that this utilitarian concept was far from the egoistic exploitation which had characterized French colonization heretofore.[50] Harmand was not returning to the *Pacte coloniale;* he was rather pointing the way to the idea of *mise en valeur* as later developed by Albert Sarraut.[51]

The utility which the mother country sought in her overseas regions was to be derived from the prosperity of the regions themselves and through the satisfaction of the natives' wants and aspirations. This policy was the repudiation of France's "parasitic" policy, and, moreover, the way to avoid repetition of earlier abuses, Harmand remarked.

To vaunt our generosity incessantly, to put to the fore our democratic liberalism is not a bad idea among ourselves and can be useful. But it is far better if we try to conform our acts to the very conditions of domination by conquest. Without using these miserable hypocrisies and these "lies of civilization," which fool no one, we should seek to justify this domination by its common utility to conquerors and conquered.[52]

These dominions of which Harmand spoke at length were primarily in tropical regions and depended on native help for their improvement.[53] As Harmand imagined it, the true *colon* was the native and the *grand colonisateur* was the state.[54] The policy to be followed by the state was a policy of production, one operating on both the land and the native. With respect to the land, it was to increase the area given to economic development through the construction of public works and by means of transportation and communication. With respect to the inhabitants, it was to increase their number and their activity through good administration and good public services.[55]

Yet the question which Harmand considered all important to the organization of the dominion was that of native policy. His ideas, as already seen, led him to the policy of association which he so ardently championed. It was the emphasis which he placed on this as a policy of economic cooperation which is of interest here.

The conqueror used the native; he realized the need of the native in the economic development of the possession. Eventually the native would, therefore, reach the point of contributing beneficial assistance to the development of the dominion, the value of which he would then be able to judge.

Contrary to simple exploitation, the policy of association does not atomize the diverse native groups but rather tries to consolidate them not only for the purpose of making better use of them but also for the purpose of gaining their willing cooperation.[56] When efforts to better the social and intellectual status of the natives are included, the idea of association becomes the "best of plans." [57]

Even though the economic purposes of overseas expansion were of capital importance to him, Harmand did not write very much on the subject. Problems of colonial government and administration far more attracted his attention. It remained for Joseph Chailley-Bert to explore more fully the economic aspects of the current colonial problem.

Views of Chailley-Bert

No one worked with more diligence to defend the colonial cause than did Chailley-Bert. Seemingly ubiquitous, he traveled widely within France in order to discuss colonial matters with his fellow Frenchmen, and he also took advantage of several opportunities to visit Europe's overseas possessions. Although he wrote no definitive study of colonial policy,[58] he created an important body of doctrine through his articles and his speeches.

His declarations touching upon the political and cultural importance of overseas France were indeed numerous,[59] but he did not hide the fact that he placed chief emphasis on the economic importance of the empire. From this point radiated important lines of his thought.

In contrast to many of his contemporaries, Chailley-Bert did not believe that the colonies had to "pay" immediately. The claim made by Jules Ferry that the colonies would provide available new markets was deceiving.[60] In truth, the consumers of French products did not yet exist in the overseas regions. This fact did not mean, however, that Ferry was wrong, continued Chailley-Bert. He was simply some fifty years ahead of schedule: the principle was correct; the timing was bad. According to Chailley-Bert every society passed through successive stages of development running the gamut from the pastoral and agricultural to the commercial and the industrial.[61] At the moment the French possessions were in the "age of agriculture." [62]

Backing up his contentions with reference to evolutionary doctrine, he asserted that nothing the French could do would change the order of a region's economic development.[63] In effect the French possessions contained peoples at the threshold of civilization and consequently their economy was agrarian. Commerce and industry would come later, at which time these regions would be rich and therefore in a position to consume French products.[64]

This miscalculation which Chailley-Bert saw in the evaluation of the economic status of the French empire was matched by one in the explanation of the empire itself. He stressed the point that the empire could be considered a *Plus Grande France*, but not a *Nouvelle France*.[65] The possessions recently acquired in no way resembled either France's former colonial domain or continental France itself. Instead of *colonies à peupler* France had acquired *possessions à administrer*.[66] What was needed in the possessions were not large numbers of Frenchmen but rather a limited number of specialized colonists and a large quantity of capital.[67]

However, because of the lack of clear understanding of this distinction, the tendency had developed in France to apply indifferently domestic laws to overseas regions without much consideration of the distinctive characteristics of each region. While such practices could have been tolerated in previous centuries when the colonies contained a larger number of Frenchmen, any thought in this direction today, cautioned Chailley-Bert, would have to be discarded. In particular, the theory of the colonies *en bloc* had to be refuted.[68]

Consideration of the colonial empire as a unified whole had been fostered by many imperialists whose enthusiasm for the colonial cause led them to plead for the empire as if it were a single, large unit. Chailley-Bert admonished his confederates for this practice, and he indicated that he personally deplored the "terrible habit" of admiring the colonies without distinction and of thinking of "undertaking to improve them all in equal manner and at the same time." [69]

The problem had stemmed from an error of language, and this error of language engendered an error of policy. Possessions were erroneously treated as colonies; they received French legislation which was scarcely changed for their benefit. Here was a fact which seemed uniquely French, Chailley-Bert remarked. German and Dutch authors "are astonished at our confusion of language, the source of our errors in practice. The English would never permit such a theory of uniformity with regard to their colonies." [70]

In order to avoid these mentioned pitfalls in the future, Chailley-Bert thought that France should begin to practice indirect colonial rule through a policy of decentralization, which he considered the first rule of good colonial administration. The sole task of the mother country under such a program would be to choose able governors who would be given wide discretionary powers. In fact, he insisted: "Intervention is stagnation, perhaps death. Decentralization is progress and life." [71] Within the possession itself an indirect method of rule was the best, he believed. No longer were the French colonists to take possession of native land, but rather they were to encourage indirect cooperation. The Frenchman would abstain from all direct participation in the development of the country, while this process of development itself would be designed to serve France's industrial interests.[72]

At this point one approaches what is perhaps the key idea in the colonial theory created by Chailley-Bert. This is a native policy closely linked with the economic need for overseas expansion.

Chailley-Bert contended that the objectives and nature of colonial policy in the nineteenth century gave a new orientation to native policy, one contrasting with that of the older expansion when *colonies de peuplement* were chiefly sought.[73] Now nations were only seeking clients and subjects, and these they found chiefly in the tropics, regions populated by peoples of old and refined civilizations whose attachment to outdated forms of thought and government alone had made them prey to the invading European nations.[74] The chief goal of the European powers was to retain these clients and subjects, to increase their number and their wealth and, by so doing, to increase their own benefits since the subject peoples would then be able to buy more and pay more taxes. In addition to this economic boon the European powers might well begin agricultural and industrial enterprises, although such activities could only take place with the support of the natives, for the climate forbade European labor. The European "brings the techniques and the capital; the soil furnishes the raw materials; the native alone supplies the labor." [75] For these reasons the native becomes "a source of wealth, an agent of production, a collaborator." [76]

Two ideas dominated the new native policy which Chailley-Bert envisaged.[77] The first, previously explained by Gustave Le Bon, asserted that education could not quickly transform the mentality of a people. Hence centuries would be required before the native masses could understand and imitate the European. The second, following from the first, was that European civilization could not be made immediately accessible to the natives and might even be dangerous for them. Thus if the natives were to be helped by the European, the process would have to follow native lines, not European ones. Cautioned Chailley-Bert: "Let's start from that which they accept and know, and proceed with extreme slowness toward that which we know and accept." [78] A practical program, good government and a paternal administration were needed, and the results of these would be increased wealth and contentment among the native population, meaning increased benefits for the occupying power. But here once more Chailley-Bert insisted the results would demand considerable time.[79]

Expressed in other terms this program consisted in the policy of association to which Chailley-Bert gave his own explanation:

This policy of association rests on the idea that the natives are, at least provisionally, inferior to the Europeans, or at least different, that they have their past, their customs, their institutions and a religion to which they adhere. Even with the aid of education their minds cannot understand and accept our concepts any more rapidly. But it is the duty of the stronger people to guide the weaker people, to aid them in the evolution of their own civilization, until that day when they are close enough to ours so that they may take from it what they deem good. While awaiting this result of education and of time, we must respect their ideas, their customs, religion and civilization.[80]

The economic interpretation given by Chailley-Bert to overseas expansion and to native policy was no doubt the chief reason, or at least the most ostensible one, for his support of the policy of association. As he said, France, in dealing with the native populations, "must aim at associating them first with her economic undertakings and later with the task of government." [81]

The relationship between the avowed economic necessity of French expansion and the policy of association thus appears to be a quite simple one. It was also a very practical one. As interpreters of France's economic problems, the colonial theorists advocating association were not motivated principally by stimulating ideals but by the more basic desire of making the overseas possessions into those markets deemed necessary for France's well-being. Thus the more rapidly and easily this goal was achieved, the better for France.

Although the economic reasons mentioned above were the most often given for acceptance of the policy of association, there were others, of course. As the impact of the social sciences and studies of comparative colonization turned France's colonial theorists in this new direction, so did—even if to a much lesser degree—the military problems of the day.

Chapter 8

MILITARY PROBLEMS AND THE
POLICY OF ASSOCIATION

AT the beginning of the twentieth century the problem of the defense of France's overseas possessions was formulated in a new fashion, the results of which were to influence colonial theory. Until the end of the nineteenth century and the pacification of Madagascar, military efforts in the French colonial empire were almost entirely devoted to the pacification of these regions officially annexed but in reality still not completely subdued. Henceforth, however, military concerns were of another and more serious nature. The possibility of attack from the outside became apparent.

The real cause of this new orientation of colonial military strategy is to be found in the surge of imperialism itself. The appetite of European nations—and also non-European nations, for the United States and Japan were engaged in the imperialistic race—for new overseas possessions led to numerous international rivalries and several threats of war. In this tumultuous world climate the Fashoda incident was but one storm.

As a result of this activity, after 1900 some French colonial experts showed considerable interest in military matters. The famous expression, "the fate of our colonies will be decided on the Rhine," [1] might have seemed a justification for not undertaking a strong defense of the overseas possessions. Yet, because of the very size of the French empire and its exposed boundaries, a colonial war could very easily have broken out. In such a situation the French navy and army could not have been expected to guarantee ample defense on short notice.

Besides these considerations the efficacy of the colonial army was not estimated very highly because of its system of recruitment. According to the law of July 30, 1893, this army could only recruit its French troops by way of enlistment.[2] Its numbers were, unfortunately, far below those needed for colonial military defense. This fact was largely responsible for the belief, fostered by imperialists and military authorities alike, that the role played by the native in the defense of his own soil would have to be enlarged. Heretofore, each colonial military unit had, in theory, been composed of a proportion of two Europeans for three natives. But faced with a well-equipped, well-trained enemy, such a small army would scarcely have been able to defend the area assigned to it. With this condition in mind one writer remarked: "We are too timorous in our use of natives." [3] A proportion of one European for two natives or even, eventually, one European for ten natives was demanded.[4] Such talk indicated to those persons concerned with colonial military problems that only with the support of pacified native populations would France arrive at some concrete solution to the problem, and this solution was to be nothing less than the autonomous defense of each colony.[5]

Everyone interested in the issue seemed to be in agreement on the matter. In several speeches to the Société africaine de France, Ferdinand de Béhagle and Paul Bourdarie emphasized the importance of an "association" between native and *colon* for military reasons.[6] Le Myre de Vilers, reporter of the budget for the colonies in 1900, said: "The defense of the colonies is far more a question of administration and native policy than it is a military question."[7] The Colonial Congress of Marseilles in 1906 passed the following resolution: "Resolved: that the natives be utilized to the greatest extent possible from the military point of view; that native troops constitute the basis of the military forces charged with the defense of our overseas possessions."[8] In order to escape from any possible internal dangers resulting from such a proposed policy, the Congress added that it was necessary "to follow a native policy intelligently conceived in order to make our domination agreeable."[9]

The "Yellow Peril"

All of these ideas suggested the reasons for the growth of interest in a policy of association related to military matters. But it was a growing fear of the supposed "yellow peril" which accelerated the acceptance of the policy. In the words of one Frenchman: "At last we have a native policy of association. . . . It took the far-reaching events of the Russo-Japanese War to demonstrate the urgent necessity of it." [10]

The Russo-Japanese War dramatically announced the arrival of Japan among the world's great powers and, to a degree, announced the awakening of the Orient from its centuries-long political dormancy. The colonial powers of Europe, fearing even a struggle between races,[11] were disturbed by this astonishing fact and began to regard their far-flung possessions situated in the Pacific, and hence close to Japan, nervously.

In France the problem was essentially that of the defense of Indochina. Not only were the imperialists particularly anxious about France's position in Asia because of the unexpected turn of the Russo-Japanese War, but they were also distressed by the revelation of a supposedly confidential Japanese military report, the authorship of which had been attributed to Lieutenant-General Baron Kodama, governor of Formosa in 1902. In this interesting document, published in the *Echo de Paris* in January 1905,[12] Baron Kodama outlined Japan's program for aggressive expansion. Suggesting that his country ought to attack first in the direction of the north where the adversary was more immediate and also more vulnerable, he insisted, however, on the necessity of Japan's turning thereafter toward the south and Indochina, "our future possession." [13] Nevertheless, according to the Kodama report, it would be advisable for Japan to wait until 1908 for this latter venture, because at that time "Indochina, then organized and endowed with all the means of production, would be worth the conquest." [14] Moreover, Formosa, then completely pacified, could be used as a jumping-off place.

It is quite obvious that, faced with a militarily victorious Japan in 1906 and with a supposedly confidential report that spelled possible doom for French Indochina, the French imperialists interested in Indochina were distressed and asked themselves how the possession could be effectively defended. [15]

In addition, this anxiety was stimulated by a growing fear arising from the state of China. On the one hand certain Frenchmen believed that the Japanese would make use of the Chinese in the large army with which they supposedly planned to force the Europeans out of Asia. [16] On the other hand, a horror of an "awakened giant" existed in the hearts of some Frenchmen: if China found a strong government and armed herself rapidly, "it is certain that the three hundred million industrious and ingenious inhabitants who people its fertile territory would offer ample resources for the creation of a formidable military empire." [17] Already it was thought that certain Chinese mandarins were in the process of creating for themselves a strong army which would immediately threaten the existence of Indochina. [18]

Whatever their intrinsic value, these thoughts on the "yellow peril" at least aroused French interest in the native problem in Indochina. The French Parliament, in order to study the defense of that region, sent the deputy from Indochina, François Deloncle, on an inspection trip in 1905.

Upon his return Deloncle emphasized the imperative necessity of gaining native cooperation for the defense of the
country.[19] This could be accomplished, he thought, by the
adaptation of local French administration to the habits and
mentality of the local inhabitants.

In a similar vein Henri Lorin, Professor of Colonial
Geography at the University of Bordeaux, wrote that the
best defense of Indochina was a sound native policy. "If
our subjects believe us to be sincere and sympathetic pro-
tectors and allies, they will willingly serve us and fight, if
need be, for themselves and for us." [20] Finally, the Minister
of Colonies, Clémentel, referring to the policy of association, affirmed that by being generous and humane, France
would solve the problem of the defense of her overseas
possessions.[21]

The Opinions of Albert de Pouvourville

The policy of association was thus touched upon in military matters, but it was Albert de Pouvourville who tied
it so closely to the defense of Indochina. An expert in problems of the Far East, Pouvourville had a literary career
which was extremely productive of novels and poetry as
well as of political and economic works. His contribution
to the thought about the native problem was but a small
part of his work on Asia.[22]

The theme of his *Les Défenses de l'Indo-Chine et la
politique d'association* was inspired by the report of the
Deloncle mission to Indochina. Pouvourville concurred in

the thought that the political evolution in the Far East necessitated a new and more efficacious policy in Indochina. In particular, he feared the ambitions of Japan, a nation which "owes it to itself and to the yellow race to chase the white invaders from Asiatic soil." [23]

The military problem consequently concerned Pouvourville. Obviously, he wrote, it was necessary that Indochina be able to defend herself by her own means until the arrival of the French fleet which would thereupon turn the balance to France's favor. The delay which would of necessity ensue before such naval help could arrive was the principal reason for which close cooperation of the native in military matters was of paramount interest.[24]

No question in colonial matters seemed more important to Pouvourville. The very distance of the colonies from continental France implied that no defense was possible if the local population was not associated with the French efforts. Instead of making them "passive instruments," France had to make the natives "intelligent and voluntary collaborators." [25] And in order to attain this goal French-native cooperation had to be extended beyond the military sphere to include all aspects of native life. In short, according to Pouvourville, a complete renovation of French colonial policy in Indochina was necessary. This was his reason for arguing in favor of a policy of association, which he declared was not "a simple attempt of our civilizing efforts . . . but the ineluctable condition of French power in Indochina." [26]

The opposite of the doctrine of assimilation,[27] the policy of association, Pouvourville insisted, attempted to adapt French methods to the temperament of the native race. Government authority and the general direction of the possession's affairs were to remain within complete French control, but this was all.[28] In other matters all that which was not contrary to the purposes of French colonial objectives was not to be altered.[29] The manner in which this policy was to operate was explained by Pouvourville as follows:

When they leave the level of general institutions, French preoccupations must, in becoming particular, be Indochinese preoccupations. When it leaves the level of conception and goes to the level of application, national policy must become local policy. And when it leaves regulatory legal principles to become particular measures, French administration must be native administration.[30]

Thus if general policy was restricted to French authority, political and economic activity on the local level was to be primarily the concern of the native. Support for this administration was to be obtained from those native elements which would be best able to interpret French directions according to popular native sentiments. These persons were the native leaders who, well versed in local institutions, would become the necessary and true collaborators of the French.

The recognition and acceptance of these chief points by the French implied that French administrators would henceforth have to act in accordance with the characteristics of native mentality so that they would be able to determine in what manner "the traditional native foundation and imported French civilization must unite in order to bring together all energies for the true national goal" in Indochina.[31]

Pouvourville followed his general remarks with definite suggestions about the means by which his program could be achieved. Among other things he suggested that the importance of traditionalism in Annamite life be recognized, that the method of recruiting administrative personnel from among the native aristocracy be retained, that all judicial matters strictly pertaining to the native be left in the hands of native authorities and that the "communism" of communal life be left unaltered.[32]

On every level of native existence, cooperation and adaptation, based on respect for local institutions and the traditional spirit of the people, would be so reinforced that the natives would soon be convinced of the value of the French occupation.[33]

Endowed with a sound policy of association, Indochina would be able to acquire an effective military organization and one in which the native, not the European, would play the dominant role. The French could have confidence in the native, added Pouvourville, because he would be acquainted with the reasons for which such a defense was imperative. Organized into military reserves based on local custom and needs, trained according to war "in the manner of the yellow races" and not according to the type of combat characteristic of colonial skirmishes,[34] the native would render great service to the French and, of course, to the defense of the colony.

The essential idea of the points discussed above was summarized by Pourvourville at the French Colonial Congress of 1905. He produced a "utilitarian syllogism": "We have need of the cooperation of the native forces; we can only obtain these forces by adapting our methods to the traditions, ideas and temperament of the race; therefore, let's accept the traditions, adopt the ideas, and take advantage of the temperament." [35]

Associate the native with the rights and duties of the French in his country—this was Pouvourville's goal. The rights implied the economic and moral betterment of the country; the duties implied the creation of a native army.[36]

In 1912 General Pennequin, commander-in-chief of the army in Indochina, corroborated the ideas held by Pouvourville. Favoring the creation of a native army, he lamented the fact that the French had not yet won the native population over to the colonial cause. Native support was necessary to safeguard the colony. As he wrote:

Association and collaboration have often been spoken of. These are generous ideas emanating from France, but here how little they are realized. . . .

First, what is needed is a real policy of association; we must educate the Annamites and give them access to all positions. There must no longer be conquerors and conquered here, but all, Annamites and Frenchmen, must be part of the same empire.[37]

In the opinion of some theorists the military necessity of the policy of association extended beyond the geographical limits suggested by Pouvourville and Pennequin. Not only the "yellow peril" but all possibilities of military difficulties in the colonies might be avoided thanks to this policy.

"Against the yellow or the black peril, a better remedy could not be found." [38] Thus what was suggested for Indochina was also suggested for Africa.[39] The employment of Negro troops was not a new idea, of course. The *Tirailleurs sénégalais*, organized by Faidherbe, had already demonstrated how valuable native troops might be. What was important, however, was the additional emphasis that the military problem gave to the native problem and the need for its resolution.

Chapter 9

IDEAL AND REALITY

AFTER all was said and done, what effect did the changes in doctrine and theory evidenced during the period under study have on French colonial policy? The question is both interesting and provocative, for French colonial history following the First World War indicates that a simple answer is impossible. Even though association became the official colonial policy immediately after the war,[1] the ghost of assimilation lingered on and could still be seen flitting in and out of French colonial affairs. Yet observation of this activity does not permit one to conclude that the French always uphold the old maxim, *Plus ça change, plus c'est la même chose.*

It is clear that most of the French colonial theorists and popularizers in metropolitan France did consciously set aside the doctrine of assimilation and did uphold association in some form or other. The support they obtained for their stand was ample, as has been seen. But ever present in French colonial theory was the moral element, the responsibility which the conqueror assumed toward the conquered and without which many felt the conquest could not be justified. Around this issue association and indeed assimilation were often centered and hence at times tended to overlap.

Quite frankly, some of the imperialists of the period actually believed that association was but a thin guise for assimilation. One writer stated: "Thanks to the ambiguous sentimentality upon which the policy of association is based, one has seen the policy of assimilation, thus disguised, recommence its destructive work on native institutions." [2] Charles Régismanset, who condemned all colonial doctrine in the years before the First World War, wrote that association "which, on the whole, leans toward the same objective as its predecessor [assimilation] but which is a little more tainted with sentimental and humanitarian preoccupations, isn't worth any more than its predecessor. It is even inferior because of the cloak of hypocrisy with which it is clothed." [3]

But even the avowed advocates of association were willing to admit that their policy contained inherent dangers. Jules Harmand had carefully stated that association "can be used as a perfected weapon in favor of assimilation, an attempt to remake for this old passion a new virginity." [4] Although Harmand had emphasized the need for improvement of the native's intellectual and social status as part of the task of imperialism, he did fear the possible effects of France's tendency toward assimilation.[5]

The fear was justified, for this moral obligation attributed by so many imperialists to the act of overseas expansion paved the way for a reappearance of assimilation in the context of colonial theory.

This fact is noticeable in the thoughts of Leopold de Saussure. Saussure, author of *La Psychologie de la coloni-*

sation française, was one of the first to attack assimilation strongly, to "prove" its invalidity according to Spencerian ideas.[6] Yet within five years of the publication of his sensational book, he was explaining how the assimilation of the natives could be accomplished by the French. Saussure, however, did differentiate between assimilation based on "realities and experience" and assimilation "from the point of view of unitary traditions which encourage proselytism by language, morals and institutions."[7] The former type was the one he favored. He characterized it by the improvement of the *condition morale* of the native, by his intellectual betterment and transformation.[8]

For Saussure the sole method by which the native ought to be assimilated was one which stemmed from the belief that no universally applicable rules existed in such matters. Each instance was different and necessitated study of the natives' environment and past before any attempt at transformation of institutions could be chanced. Hence the difficulties previously encountered by the French were a result more of their false ideas about human nature than of actual social conditions.[9] What Saussure was arguing for was modified assimilation rather than *assimilation à outrance*. Still one can ask where the line was to be drawn.

Saussure was not alone in holding these beliefs. Numerous imperialists talked of the need for "tutelage" in colonial matters.[10] The very idea of one nation imposing her will on another carried with it a picture of some sort of superior-inferior relationship, and the one of teacher-pupil was very appealing to the French mind. Again, the concern about moral obligations made itself felt and obviously influenced the interpretation of association being fostered. The possible correlation of association with assimilation was at one point made in this fashion: "The colonies request to be assimilated to the mother country, but this assimilation must be made in the sense that it carries with it the association of the natives with our activities." [11]

Now return to 1889 and the ideas expressed by Senator Issac at the National Colonial Congress of that year. Issac wanted assimilation and strongly demanded that it remain France's official colonial policy. But he never suggested that total assimilation should be attempted immediately. He stated that no society could be suddenly changed by a *coup de baguette*. Change was to be wrought with "prudence, with slowness, especially with benevolence." [12] It would immediately seem, therefore, that the colonial theories held by Issac were not so far removed from those of Saussure or, for that matter, from those expressed by most of the supporters of association.[13]

Movement away from assimilation was difficult at times. And here was a problem not restricted to the French alone. All colonial powers practiced assimilation in some form or other.[14] The French, however, were the ones who did it most consciously. Yet how could such a policy be totally avoided? It almost seems a concomitant feature of the act of overseas expansion and for reasons other than the moral one suggested above.

Of considerable importance in the formation of such an attitude and the tendency toward such a practice is the nature of the relationship of conqueror and conquered. The success of the conquest itself suggested the superiority of the conqueror, the weakness of the conquered. And thanks to the egoism of man, to this force that sociologists call ethnocentrism, the processes and institutions deemed necessary for the development of the possession and the betterment of its inhabitants were those of the "mother country." In spite of the best intentions of many imperialists it was difficult to think otherwise. Even a people like the English, lauded for their practical nature and condemned for their supposed coldness toward their colonial peoples, had succumbed to a form of assimilation in India.[15]

The state of European civilization at the end of the nineteenth century enhanced the ethnocentric spirit of the European colonial. Blessed with material advantages scarcely known to most regions of the world, the European judged other peoples by his own measures. Not a cephalic index but a standard-of-living index was most commonly employed, for, all too often, civilization and material progress were used as interchangeable terms. As Pierre Mille had sarcastically written in condemnation of this attitude: "The Chinese, having no railroads, no mechanical textile industry, no Napoleon, and no Moltke are extremely inferior to us." [16]

If the French were assimilators at heart, they were, nevertheless, not alone. Yet the adoption of any new colonial theory or policy in France was definitely hindered by this dominant attitude.

Nor should it be overlooked that assimilation was not

strictly unilateral. Native populations, initially awed and fascinated by the imposing appearance of the European and the material proof of the high degree of his own cultural attainment, often sought to emulate him. The imitation of European dress is but one obvious example, as was the practice of wealthy natives of sending their children, whenever possible, to good European schools. And it is as ironic as it is true that the most successful aspect of assimilation, realized in our own times, was not sought by the imperialistic powers—the nationalism drawn along Western lines now evident in most of the former colonial regions of the world.

The attitude and problem of the native populations might be summed up in the words of Leopold Senghor: "Assimiler, sans être assimilés."

Finally, it should be emphasized that association, whenever seen to embrace the idea of the protectorate, had its own difficulties. Too easily the protectorate devolved from an international arrangement providing for the coexistence of two different peoples into a type of direct rule scarcely hidden behind the pretension of continued native administration. At the top echelons the French substituted their own rule for that of the existing government so that association only really worked on a limited local level.[17]

Assimilation, consciously or unconsciously pursued, haunted those French theorists who turned toward some form of association as an answer to the native problem. Even as recently as the debates over the constitution of the Fourth Republic, evidence of this can be found. And two contemporary colonial theorists demonstrate that the opponents and admirers of assimilation have not all receded into the depths of history. Speaking about assimilation in 1954, Paul Mus, former director of the Ecole nationale de la France d'Outre-Mer, declared: "When our policy of gallicanization and cultural uprooting leads to the disintegration of African society, it violates sacred values which, for every people, are an unalienable right. In destroying them French policy defies God as well as man." [18] A more generous attitude toward assimilation is that of Hubert Deschamps, himself a former governor-general and now a professor at the Institut d'Etudes politiques of the University of Paris. Considering assimilation a part of the French intellectual tradition, he saw this policy as an ennobling one, reflecting the belief in the unity of mankind.[19]

The discussion carried on between 1890 and 1914, like the opinions expressed above, was more than academic. The interest in policy which led to changes in theory did have a salubrious effect. As one author put it, changes were felt on the periphery.[20] More autonomy in regional affairs became evident, and the acceptance of a more flexible colonial policy by the officials in Paris did result. Not least of all, a keener interest in the overseas empire and its multitudinous problems was aroused.

A concept of the role to be played by the native elite in this system of indirect rule, which association largely was, also emerged and has a thread of history leading down to the present, with an interesting knot appearing in the Brazzaville Conference of 1944 when the ideas of Félix

Eboué, governor of French Equatorial Africa, threw additional light on the advantages to be derived from the use of the native elite.[21] Of course the importance of the native elite in the policy of association is self-evident. As one French writer said in a discussion of association: "It requires that the upper classes—that is, the elite—participate in public affairs and retain the social rank they have acquired." [22] They were to be the go-betweens for the French and the native populations. Quite an ambitious native role, imagined along these lines, appeared in the thoughts of the deputy A. Messimy, who in a report to the Chamber of Deputies in July, 1912, spoke of the French need to draw more closely the more assimilated elements within the growing Algerian population.

It is by this slow fusion of the elite and by the association of the rest of the population with our interests that the Algeria of tomorrow will grow, drawing in its wake all of this North Africa where the France of the future will tap a new source of vigor.[23]

Of course attendant problems to which Messimy did not allude were bound to arise. The problem of the *déraciné* is the most important, and it is one which still hounds the French in their remaining overseas territories.

Placed between a native society living in a static condition for centuries and failing to see the need for changing whatever its manner of living, working and acting, and between the colonizing elements who find it very convenient to live and act under a regime of pure domination which brings exclusive advantages, the men of the native elite are subject to rejection by the one group and are repulsed by the other. And it requires a very great civic courage to bear the anathema of the former and the repeated outrages and injuries of the other.[24]

Even with these evident problems clearly in view, the theorists in France still found association appealing. It could be made to work more readily than assimilation, no doubt. Adaptable it was. That one finds references to the *doctrine de l'assimilation* but references only to the *politique d'association* may be an indication of this. For one of the fundamental aims of the French imperialists engaged in discussion of colonial policy was to remove rigid doctrine from colonial matters. Even though association was not considered by all French colonial theorists to be a blanket solution for all French colonial relationships, it was suggested for those areas most likely to be immediately productive and valuable: Indochina and North Africa. Indochina in particular was singled out.

The truth of the matter is that a considerable gap always existed between whatever theories and practices were formulated in metropolitan France and the practices which were followed in the overseas regions. It would be grossly unfair to accuse the French of completely succumbing to an *idée fixe* and being guided by it as if it were a North Star of the first magnitude. The French were probably as expedient as any other colonizing power, and almost any period of French colonial history reveals a variety of practices in the then existing possessions.

Even so, the appeal of assimilation to the French mind

cannot be denied. That the elevation of French subjects to French citizens with all the rights thereby to be enjoyed most often did not happen—note the dreadful inconsistencies in the history of Algeria—does not tarnish any of the glitter of the doctrine. The same noble conception of mankind which gave to Stoic thought its appeal is to be found in the French idea of colonial assimilation. But perhaps the French were tempted to forget that Man is really men, and that the integrity of the individual must be respected.

In any event imperialism did not occur by invitation but by force, and in the long run, all noble doctrines considered, was only successful so long as this *ultima ratio* was apparent. The humanitarianism underlying the theory of assimilation seldom thrived in such an atmosphere. Not that French civilization meant to the native the rattle of the *mitrailleuse*, as some unfriendly critics would have it, but it seldom meant equality and fraternity. The native was more often exploited or ignored than he was educated. And without this latter quality assimilation was but a hollow sham. Does this then mean that assimilation was only a rationalization for outright exploitation? It may well have served such a purpose, but to insist that it served no other is to deny the French one of their more engaging qualities. No doubt cultural imperialism is part of the French tradition, and assimilation can be considered one aspect of it, even though sporadically practiced. The appeal of assimilation was genuine and was genuinely French.

To suggest that the policy of association was solely the result of a business psychology which emphasized economy of operation in order to assure increased profits is to ignore many of the purposes and sentiments of the French colonial theorists. They were not businessmen. As experienced administrators, as patriots, and as reasonable individuals, they wished to arrive at a native policy which would make the overseas empire a viable institution, one which would be of value to France. Association had great appeal because it answered many needs.

Whatever else, the discussion of doctrine and theory at the end of the nineteenth century and the beginning of the twentieth did awaken the French to the problems of modern imperialism and particularly to those concerning native policy. The importance of a method, a "science" of colonialism, as it were, designed to fuse the interests of the two peoples placed in contact by the act of imperialism itself, was henceforth recognized. And if the natives were still not treated as peers, their institutions and ways were generally more respected. The history of imperialism is too often written as a study in black and white; much of the French activity was in the grey zone where black and white are not distinguishable.

The French imperialists knew that the overseas regions would eventually break their political ties with metropolitan France, and many thought this would occur sooner than need be if assimilation were to be the accepted colonial theory. Yet this future problem, whatever its imagined immediate causes, was of little concern to contemporary imperialists. The theorists hoped to forge a sound economic link which would not give way during eventual political storms. In this matter association appeared to be promising. Whether the theorists and writers of the day were correct or not in so thinking, they were right about the political evolution of the overseas empire, albeit their timing was bad.

At present the French overseas empire is in the last stages of total disintegration. Colonialism, even if it is the most generous in the world, sows the seeds of its own destruction. The generation of colonial nationalism, though an anachronism in this age of political monoliths, is noticeable everywhere in the French overseas possessions, present and former. From Indochina to North Africa and even to the regions of Central Africa, the reaction against imperialism has had an almost catalytic effect. The day of colonial empires is certainly past.

The French colonial theorists who expressed their views on colonial developments in the years between 1890 and 1914 would no doubt be sorely disappointed if they were still alive today, but they probably would not be greatly astonished. Their own discussion of colonial theory was only an initial effort to study and solve those problems which have been present in all their acuity until our own day.

NOTES

Chapter 1. The Climate of French Colonialism

1. For an analysis of Ferry's colonial policy, see Power, *Jules Ferry and the Renaissance of French Imperialism.*

2. Even Hobson, whose economic interpretation of imperialism has become the classic one, suggests that the initiation of expansion was often the work of people devoid of economic motives. *Imperialism, A Study,* p. 59.

3. See Deschamps, *Méthodes et doctrines coloniales de la France,* pp. 152–53. Article 33 of this law stated that all revenues collected by the colonies would be left at their disposition; in turn, the colonies would henceforth be expected to shoulder their own regular expenses.

4. For the French Socialist point of view, see Louis, "Le Socialisme et l'expansion coloniale contemporaine," *Revue socialiste,* May, 1889.

5. Weinstein, *Jean Jaurès, a Study of Patriotism in the French Socialist Movement,* pp. 143–46.

6. The most important were the *Dépêche coloniale* and the *Revue indigène.*

7. Among these were the French Colonial Congresses held annually between 1903 and 1908, the International Congress of Sociology held in Paris in 1900, and the Colonial Congress of Marseilles, 1906.

8. On the activities and influence of the geographical societies, see Murphy, *The Ideology of French Imperialism,* and McKay, "Colonialism in the French Geographical Movement, 1871–1881," *Geographical Review,* XXXIII (1943), 214–32.

9. See "L'Union coloniale française: les dix premières années," *Bulletin de l'Union coloniale française* (January, 1923), p. 1.

10. A description of these organizations is given by Le Herissé in his report on the colonial budget in *Documents parlementaires, Chambre des Députés, Journal Officiel, 1903*, pp. 1563–68.

11. By 1914 the Deutsche Kolonial-Gesellschaft had several hundred thousand members. See Roberts, *History of French Colonial Policy, 1870–1925*, I, 31.

12. No adequate biography of Etienne has yet appeared. A good collection of his speeches and writings is *Eugène Etienne, son oeuvre coloniale, algérienne et politique, 1881–1906.*

13. The most interesting personalities participating in colonial group were: Théophile Delcassé (Minister of Colonies, 1894–95); François de Mahy (deputy from Réunion, Minister of Marine and Colonies, 1887–88); Etienne; Le Myre de Vilers (former resident of Madagascar); and Admiral Vallon (former governor of the Senegal).

14. The librarian of the Bibliothèque de l'Assemblée nationale informed the author of this fact. Charles-André Julien, Professor at the University of Paris, confirmed it. M. Julien believes that the activities of the colonial group were of great importance. An attempt to appraise the group is found in Brunschwig, "Le Parti colonial français," *Revue française d'histoire d'outre-mer*, XLVI (1959), 49–83. Brief accounts of the group's activities can also be found in the *Bulletin du Comité de l'Afrique française* and in *Questions diplomatiques et coloniales.*

15. Guyot, *Lettres sur la politique coloniale*, p. 215.

16. Arnaud and Méray, *Les Colonies françaises, organisation administrative, judiciaire, politique et financière*, p. 4.

17. See Deschamps, *Méthodes et doctrines coloniales de la France*, p. 214.

Chapter 2. Origins and Growth of the French Doctrine of Assimilation

1. A general survey of this and other colonial theories is to be found in Maunier, *The Sociology of Colonies*, ed. and trans. by Lorimer.

2. See Barker, "The Conception of Empire," in Bailey, ed., *The Legacy of Rome*, p. 51.

3. Cited in Rolland and Lampué, *Précis de législation coloniale*, p. 200.

4. See Deschamps, *Méthodes et doctrines coloniales de la France*, pp. 30–31.

5. See, for instance, Chailley-Bert, *Dix années de politique coloniale*, p. 49.

6. On colonial policy during the revolutionary period, see Lokke, *France and the Colonial Question* and Gaffarel *La Politique coloniale en France de 1789 à 1830.*

7. On this particular subject, see Garrett, *The French Colonial Question 1789–1791*, pp. 35–58.

8. Lokke, *France and the Colonial Question*, pp. 128–30.

9. The short-lived decree of May 15, 1791 (abrogated on September 24, 1791) might be considered of an assimilative nature. In declaring that men of property, regardless of color, were to have the right to vote, the decree prepared the way for the egalitarian aspect of colonial assimilation. Lokke wrote that granting of rights to a few would lead to similar demands by mulattoes and slaves ". . . until the Rousseau doctrine of popular sovereignty would reign in pristine purity." Lokke, *France and the Colonial Question*, p. 139. It should be noted that the Convention proclaimed the abolition of slavery on February 4, 1794.

10. Cited by Deschamps, *Méthodes et doctrines coloniales de la France*, p. 89.

11. *Titre premier, Division du territoire, Constitution du 5 Fructidor, An III.*

12. See Mornet, *La Pensée française du XVIIIe siècle*, p. 39.

13. *Oeuvres complètes de M. Helvétius*, Vol. V, *De l'homme*, Section X, 3.

14. *Ibid.*, Vol. III, *De l'homme*, Section II, 91.

15. Mornet, *Les Origines intellectuelles de la Révolution française*, p. 95.

16. Cited in Tardieu, *La Révolution à refaire*, I, 169.

17. For a brief history of colonial legislation during the nineteenth century, see Rolland and Lampué, *Précis de législation*

coloniale; Pety de Thozée, *Théories de la colonisation au XIXe siècle et le rôle de l'Etat dans le développement des colonies;* Deschamps, *Méthodes et doctrines coloniales de la France.*

18. Cited in Gaffarel, *La Politique coloniale en France,* p. 18.

19. Georges Hardy believed that this was the first time that "the idea of a colonial empire, of an extension of the mother country overseas" was realized. See his *Histoire de la colonisation française,* pp. 191–92.

20. Cited in Vignon, "La Politique du protectorat et l'inégalité des races," *Revue bleue,* III (March 25, 1905), 375.

21. Cited in Deschamps, *Méthodes et doctrines coloniales de la France,* p. 112.

22. Cited in Vignon, *Un Programme de politique coloniale,* p. 192.

23. On the law of 1892 and its implications, see Girault, *Colonial Tariff Policy of France,* pp. 94–109.

24. A senatorial commission of eighteen members, headed by Jules Ferry, was charged to investigate the Algerian problem. Its findings indicated the need for reform, and a decree of December 31, 1896, abrogated the *rattachements* and reinforced the authority of the governor-general.

25. See Girault, *Principes de colonisation et de législation coloniale,* pp. 61–62.

26. See Chatenet, "The Civil Service in France," in Robson, ed., *The Civil Service in Britain and France,* p. 163.

27. Pierre Lyautey, *L'Empire colonial français,* p. 104.

28. See the speech made by Gerville-Réache's son for him in which the son expressed the principal ideas of his father, "Principes de colonisation," *Congrès colonial français de 1905.*

29. Fouillée, *Education from a National Standpoint,* trans. and ed. by Greenstreet, p. 2.

30. Fouillée, *Psychologie du peuple français,* p. 178.

31. *Ibid.*

32. *Ibid.,* p. 181. An interesting contemporary statement concerning this French attitude is to be found in Lavergne, *Une Révolution dans la politique coloniale de la France,* p. 57. Professor Lavergne states that the continuation of assimilation's

appeal is a result of the French sentimental belief that Frenchmen are spontaneously liked and also a result of the fact that the French are by nature given to thinking on a universal plane.

33. Fouillée, *Psychologie du peuple français*, p. 186.

34. Michelet, *Le Peuple*, p. 246.

35. Fouillée, *Education from a National Standpoint*, p. 125.

36. Fouillée had some words on this subject also. He wrote: "We have, moreover, fallen heir to a portion of that Stoic, that Roman genius, which was perpetually translating itself into legislation. We like to make ourselves legislators, especially in the interest of humanity, quite as if we were members of the 'universal republic' . . . ." Fouillée *et al.*, *Modern French Legal Philosophy*, p. 22.

37. Pierre Lyautey, *L'Empire colonial français*, p. 94.

38. Girault, *Principes de colonisation*, p. 55.

39. Arnaud and Meray, *Les Colonies françaises*, p. 5.

40. See, for instance, Henry, "Sommes-nous des Latins?" *Questions diplomatiques et coloniales*, XVII (May 1, 1904), 657–63.

41. As examples, see Hobson, *Imperialism, a Study*, pp. 196–200, and Langer, *The Diplomacy of Imperialism*, I, 91–95.

42. James, *Parisian Sketches, Letters to the New York Herald, 1875–1876*, ed. by Edel and Linds, pp. 65–66.

43. Fouillée, *Education from a National Standpoint*, p. 6.

44. Castre, *The Ideals of France*, p. 34.

45. Hanotaux, *L'Energie française*, p. 365.

46. Demangeon, "La Politique coloniale," in Augé-Laribé *et al.*, *La Politique républicaine*, p. 467.

47. Thibaudet, *Les Idées politiques de la France*, p. 127.

48. Deschamps, *Les Méthodes et doctrines coloniales de la France*, p. 121.

49. Cited in *Recueil des délibérations du Congrès colonial national 1889–1890*, I, 15.

50. As modified, the resolution had the following clause added: "and progressively the spirit and civilization of metropolitan France," *ibid.*, p. 21.

51. Roberts, *History of French Colonial Policy*, I, 103.

Chapter 3. Ideas from Abroad

1. The following chapter is an elaboration of the author's article, "L'Influence des méthodes hollandaises et anglaises sur la doctrine coloniale française à la fin du XIXe siècle," *Cahiers d'histoire*, III (1958), 35–49.

2. The most widely used of the editions and the one henceforth cited unless otherwise indicated was the second, published in 1882.

3. Leroy-Beauileu, *De la colonisation chez les peuples modernes*, p. xiv.

4. Speech of Gustave Le Bon, cited in the *Compte-rendu du Congrès international de Paris 1889*, p. 93.

5. Denancy, *Philosophie de la colonisation*, p. 161.

6. The number of university theses on foreign colonial methods and problems is large for this period. One of the better examples is: Paul Gannay, *L'Impérialisme économique et la grande industrie anglaise*.

7. Meynier, *L'Afrique noire*, p. 253.

8. On this subject, see Whitehead, *French Reaction to American Imperialism*, and Leroy-Beaulieu, "Le Problème coloniale aux Etats-Unis," *L'Economiste français*, II (December 3, 1898), 751–53.

9. Chailley-Bert, *Java et ses habitants*, p. vii, and also his "La France en Asie," *Dépêche coloniale*, April 4, 1905. For similar ideas, see Vignon, "Les Sociétés indigènes, politique qui doivent suivre à leur égard des nations colonisatrices," *Revue scientifique*, X (February 5, 1898), 170–71.

10. Caboton, *Les Indes néerlandaises*, p. 20.

11. Leclerq, "Java et le système colonial des Hollandais," *Revue des deux mondes*, CXLIV (November 1, 1897), 172; and Vignon, "Les Sociétés indigènes, politique qui doivent suivre à leur égard des nations colonisatrices," *Revue scientifique*, X (February 5, 1898), 170.

12. Gonnaud, *La Colonisation hollandaise à Java*, p. 455. Leclerq expressed a similar thought, "Java et le système colonial

des Hollandais," *Revue des deux mondes,* CXLIV (November 1, 1897), 168.

13. See, for instance, Gonnaud, *La Colonisation hollandaise à Java,* pp. 446–47.

14. *Ibid.,* p. 447.

15. Chailley-Bert, *Java et ses habitants,* pp. 168–69.

16. *Ibid.,* p. 149.

17. An interesting evaluation of this system is to be found in Furnival, *Colonial Policy and Practice, a Comparative Study of Burma and the Netherlands India,* pp. 150–51.

18. See, for instance, the report of Van Kol in *Congrès international de sociologie coloniale,* I, 26.

19. Chailley-Bert, *Java et ses habitants,* p. 151.

20. Chailley-Bert, *La Hollande et les fonctionnaires des Indes néerlandaises,* p. 10.

21. Denancy, *Principes de la colonisation,* p. 206.

22. *Ibid.,* pp. 157–58, 205–6.

23. See, for instance, Chailley-Bert, *Java et ses habitants,* p. 194.

24. Lorin, "Les Hollandais et la politique d'association," *Dépêche coloniale,* October 24, 1905, and Gonnaud, *La Colonisation hollandaise à Java,* pp. 454–55.

25. Caboton, *Les Indes néerlandaises,* p. 19.

26. Cited in Roe, *Taine et l'Angleterre,* p. 44.

27. Boutmy, *Essai d'une psychologie politique du peuple anglais au XIXe siècle,* pp. 8–9.

28. Leclerc, *L'Education des classes moyennes et dirigeantes en Angleterre,* p. 32.

29. *Ibid.,* p. 28.

30. Boutmy, *Essai d'une psychologie,* pp. 14–15.

31. See the "Introduction" by Boutmy to Leclerc, *L'Education des classes,* and also pp. 60–65.

32. *Ibid.,* pp. 65–66.

33. Eleven editions in three years—plus one in English—and a wide variety of reviews attest to the book's widespread popularity.

34. Démolins, *A quoi tient la supériorité des Anglo-Saxons?*, p. 310.

35. "Author's Introduction to the English Edition," *Anglo-Saxon Superiority*, pp. xii–xiii, xxiv.

36. Démolins, *A quoi tient la supériorité des Anglo-Saxons?*, p. 410.

37. *Ibid.*, pp. 366–67.

38. For a critical review, see Sponck, "Français et Anglais," *Revue bleue*, VIII (July 3, 1897), 25–27.

39. Cited in Démolins, *A quoi tient la supériorité des Anglo-Saxons?*, Appendix, p. 419.

40. See particularly the critical analysis of Bérard, *L'Angleterre et l'impérialisme*, and Fouillée, "Néo-Latins et Anglo-Saxons," *Esquisse psychologique des peuples européens.*

41. Both of these terms enjoyed popularity. The older was "Greater Britain" and was coined by Sir Charles Dilke in his *Greater Britain, a Record of Travel in English-Speaking Countries during 1866 and 1867*. The idea of a *Plus Grande France* was suggested by Chailley-Bert and is developed in his "La France et la Plus Grande France," Extract from the *Revue politique et parlementaire*, August, 1902.

42. One example of this attitude is found in Greswell, *The Growth and Administration of the British Colonies, 1837–1897*, p. 9. Greswell wrote: "The Anglo-Saxon race is noted for its individualism, and in our Colonial Empire, with its wide horizons and free spirit, fostered by the freest institutions in the world, there has existed an unrivalled field for the play of individualism."

43. Seeley, *L'Expansion de l'Angleterre*, p. xxx.

44. *Ibid.*, pp. xxx–xxxi.

45. See the views of Fouillée on this subject, *Esquisse psychologique des peuples européens*, pp. 240–41.

46. Chailley-Bert, "La Politique indigène," *Revue économique internationale*, II (June 15–20, 1904), 74.

47. Valmor, *Les Problèmes de la colonisation*, p. 24.

48. See Howe, *Novels of Empire*, pp. 96 ff.

49. Ideas of this sort were expressed by Valmor, *Les Prob-*

lèmes de la colonisation, pp. i–ii; and Pouvourville, "Comment et avec qui nous défendrons l'Indo-Chine," *Congrès colonial de 1905,* p. 24.

50. On this subject, see Pierre Lyautey, *L'Empire colonial français,* p. 94; and Brunel, *L'Etat et l'individu dans la colonisation française moderne,* pp. 57–58 and 66–67.

51. See Fallot, *L'Avenir colonial de la France,* pp. 146 and 149, and Riquard, "Deux colonisations," *Dépêche coloniale,* June 7, 1897.

52. Blois, "Les Anglais dans l'Inde," *Revue bleue,* XIX (April 11, 1903), 477.

53. Bonvalot, "L'Administration coloniale anglaise," *Revue bleue,* IX (June 11, 1898), 759.

54. Giraudeau, "Politique coloniale," *Revue bleue,* VIII (December 11, 1897), 766.

55. Fallot, *L'Avenir colonial de la France,* p. 145.

56. Leroy-Beaulieu, "Les Colonies anglaises et les projets d'organisation de l'Empire britannique," *Revue des deux mondes,* CXXXIX (January 1, 1897), 122.

57. See Fallot, *L'Avenir colonial de la France,* pp. 146–47; and Eutrope, *Le Régime politique des colonies anglaises à self-government,* pp. 13–14.

58. Brunel, *L'Etat et l'individu dans la colonisation française moderne,* pp. 66–67.

59. Cultru, "Esprit de la politique indigène de l'Angleterre en Afrique occidentale," *Quinzaine coloniale* (February 10, 1914), p. 93.

60. Aubin, *Les Anglais aux Indes et en Egypte,* p. 229.

61. "Les Colonies anglaises, Rapport de M. Maurice Ordinaire," *Dépêche coloniale,* April 12, 1900.

62. Chailley-Bert, "La Politique indigène aux Indes anglaises," *Congrès colonial français de 1905,* p. 149. A somewhat similar view of English aloofness is found in Blois, "Les Anglais dans l'Inde," *Revue bleue,* XIX (April 11, 1904), 477.

63. Speech of Gustave Le Bon, cited in *Compte-rendu du Congrès colonial international de Paris 1889,* p. 75.

64. Harmand, "Préface," Strachey, *L'Inde,* p. viii. The Prince

Henri d'Orléans, also an ardent expansionist, agreed with Harmand on this point. He wrote: "For us the period of colonial conquest is over or nearly over. Now that we have conquered, we must produce, that is, gain profits. And to do that we must imitate the English who have continued the work of Dupleix." *Politique extérieure et coloniale*, p. 209.

65. Temple, *L'Inde britannique*, trans. by Siefert, p. viii.

66. See Pierre Lyautey, *L'Empire colonial français*, p. 85.

67. Chailley-Bert, *Colonisation de l'Indo-Chine, l'expérience anglaise*, pp. vi–vii.

68. *Ibid.*, pp. 3–4.   69. *Ibid.*, p. 5.

70. *Ibid.*, p. 131.   71. *Ibid.*, pp. 323–25.

72. *Ibid.*, pp. 124 ff., and pp. 319–20.

73. *Ibid.*, pp. 107–8.   74. *Ibid.*, pp. 109–10.

75. *Ibid.*, pp. 218–19.   76. *Ibid.*, p. 382.

77. *Ibid.*   78. *Ibid.*, p. 383.

79. *Ibid.*, pp. 383–92.

80. The reason for which the English had discarded the protectorate in Burma, according to Chailley-Bert, was that the "protected government was forever incapable of meeting its engagements." *Ibid.*, p. 207.

81. Harmand, "Préface," Strachey, *L'Inde*, pp. vii–ix.

82. *Ibid.*, p. viii.

83. Harmand pointed out that Indochina had a homogeneous race, whereas India did not. This implied that the French could not follow the English tactics of "divide and conquer." *Ibid.*, pp. xi–xii.

84. *Ibid.*, pp. xv–xvi.   85. *Ibid.*, pp. xviii–xix.

86. *Ibid.*, p. xxi.   87. *Ibid.*

88. *Ibid.*, pp. xxviii–xxix.   89. *Ibid.*, p. xxxii.

90. Chailley-Bert, "La Politique indigène aux Indes anglaises," *Congrès colonial français de 1905*, p. 144. On another occasion he wrote that the English had been "very mediocre colonizers" and had only recently mended their ways. "La Forme des colonies et son influence sur la législation qui leur convient," *L'Economiste français*, I (February 27, 1892), 262–64.

91. Boutmy, *Essai d'une psychologie*, p. 149.

92. Baillaud, *La Politique indigène de l'Angleterre en Afrique occidentale*, pp. 548–51.

93. "Les Colonies anglaises, Rapport de M. Maurice Ordinaire," *Dépêche coloniale*, April 12, 1900.

94. Bardoux, *L'Angleterre radicale, Essai de psychologie sociale, 1906–1913*, p. 226.

95. *Ibid.*, p. 233.   96. *Ibid.*, pp. 234–35.

97. Bérard, *L'Angleterre et l'Impérialisme*, p. 375.

98. Davray, "L'Angleterre et la prépondérance européenne," *Mercure de France*, XXXVIII (June, 1901), 659–60.

Chapter 4. Assimilation and the Scientific Attitude

1. Lamartine, *Voyage en Orient*, II, 289.

2. Gobineau, *Essai sur l'inégalité des races humaines*, I, 289.

3. Renan, *De l'origine du langage*, p. 67.

4. It is interesting to note that the *Revue internationale de sociologie*, a publication of acknowledged importance, was founded in 1890 with René Worms as its editor. Worms himself was interested in the study of native populations in the French colonies.

5. Durkheim enjoys a reputation which history has denied Fouillée, but the latter was not without influence. For an analysis of his contribution to political theory, see Scott, *Republican Ideas and the Liberal Tradition in France*, pp. 159–69.

6. Durkheim, *Règles de la méthode sociologique*, p. 8.

7. *Ibid.*, p. 105.   8. *Ibid.*, p. vii.

9. Fouillée, "Le Caractère des races humaines et l'avenir de la race blanche," *Revue des deux mondes*, CXXIV (July 1, 1894), 88.

10. *Ibid.*   11. *Ibid.*, p. 89.

12. *Ibid.*, p. 91.   13. *Ibid.*, p. 93.

14. *Ibid.*   15. *Ibid.*, p. 96.

16. See his article, "La Psychologie des peuples et l'anthropologie," *Revue des deux mondes*, CXXVIII (March 15, 1895).

17. *Psychologie du peuple français*, p. i.

18. Men of the calibre of Lucien Lévy-Bruhl were attracted

to these ideas. See particularly Lévy-Bruhl's *Les Fonctions mentales dans les sociétés inférieures,* p. 19.

19. On the question of primitive mentalities and outdated sociological theories, see the study of Mannoni, *Psychologie de la colonisation.* Lévy-Bruhl, for instance, questioned his own theories much later in his *Carnets.* Therein he stated that "from the strictly logical point of view, no essential difference is to be noted between a primitive mentality and our own." *Les Carnets de Lévy-Bruhl,* p. 70.

20. Little has been written about Le Bon. Perhaps the best brief sketch about him and his controversial nature is that of the Princess Bibesco, "Le Docteur Faust de la Rue Vignon," *Images d'Epinal.* An American evaluation of Le Bon's work is that of Barnes, "A Psychological Interpretation of Modern Sociological Problems and of Contemporary History: A Survey of the Contributions of Gustave Le Bon to Social Psychology," *American Journal of Psychology,* XXXI (1920), 333–69.

21. Le Bon, *L'Homme et les sociétés, leurs origines et leur histoire,* II, 411.

22. *Ibid.,* p. 129.   23. *Ibid.*

24. In an earlier work, *Les premières civilisations* (1889), Le Bon set forth most of the ideas contained in this book. However, the former publication was in no way as influential as the latter.

25. Le Bon, *Les Lois psychologiques de l'évolution des peuples* (1st ed.), p. 6.

26. *Ibid.,* pp. 11–12.   27. *Ibid.,* p. 12.
28. *Ibid.* (6th ed.), p. 12.   29. *Ibid.,* p. 26.
30. *Ibid.,* p. 28.   31. *Ibid.* (1st ed.), p. 35.
32. *Ibid.,* p. 3.

33. *Compte-rendu du Congrès colonial international de Paris, 1889,* p. 60.

34. *Ibid.,* p. 74.

35. See, for instance, the review by Leroy-Beaulieu, "Les Principes du régime des indigènes dans les colonies," *L'Economiste français,* II (December 2, 1899), 785–88.

36. Saussure, *La Psychologie de la colonisation française dans ses rapports avec les sociétés indigènes*, p. 1.

37. *Ibid.*, pp. 2–3.   38. *Ibid.*, p. 10.
39. *Ibid.*, p. 8.   40. *Ibid.*, p. 32.
41. *Ibid.*, p. 33.   42. *Ibid.*, p. 35.
43. *Ibid.*, p. 52.   44. *Ibid.*, p. 65.
45. *Ibid.*, p. 71.   46. *Ibid.*, pp. 75–77.
47. *Ibid.*, p. 104.   48. *Ibid.*, pp. 105–7.
49. *Ibid.*, p. 108.   50. *Ibid.*, pp. 277 ff.
51. *Ibid.*, p. 293.   52. *Ibid.*, p. 268.
53. *Ibid.*, p. 295.   54. *Ibid.*, p. 307.
55. *Ibid.*, p. 311.

56. *Congrès international de sociologie coloniale*, I, 20.

57. *Ibid.*, p. 237.   58. *Ibid.*, p. 364.

59. While he believed that absolute assimilation was undesirable, he concluded that in principle assimilation was the most desirable form of colonial policy (he had compared three forms: subjugation, autonomy, and assimilation), for, "policy of patriotic harmony, of generous brotherhood, it unites peoples while bettering them." *Principes de colonisation*, p. 5.

60. *Congrès international de sociologie coloniale*, I, 52.

61. Billiard, "Etude sur la condition politique et juridique à assigner aux indigènes des colonies," *Congrès international de sociologie coloniale*, II.

62. *Ibid.*, p. 9.   63. *Ibid.*, pp. 12–13.
64. *Ibid.*, p. 53.

65. G. Dumoutier, "De la condition morale des Annamites au Tonkin et des moyens pédagogiques d'en élever le niveau," *Congrès international de sociologie coloniale*, II, 378.

66. *Congrès international de sociologie coloniale*, I, 411 ff.

67. See the speech of Chailley-Bert at the closing banquet of the Colonial Congress of Marseilles. *Compte-rendu des travaux du Congrès colonial de Marseille*, I, 126.

68. Leroy-Beaulieu, *De la colonisation chez les peuples modernes* (6th ed.), II, 619.

69. *Ibid.*, p. 621.

70. Clozel and Villaumin, *Les Coutumes indigènes de la Côte d'Ivoire*, p. 69.

71. Lahy, "La Colonisation scientifique," *Dépêche coloniale*, February 1, 1907.

72. A variation of such thought is found in Humbert, *L'Oeuvre française aux colonies*, p. 202. In explaining why France's overseas territories should be allowed to retain their individuality, he wrote: "Their young organism cannot live the same life as the already aging organism of the mother country."

73. Valmor, *Les Problèmes de la colonisation*, pp. ii–iii.

74. Messimy, *Notre oeuvre coloniale*, p. 59.

75. Giran, *De l'éducation des races*, pp. vii–viii.

76. *Ibid.*, p. 8.   77. *Ibid.*, p. 5.

78. *Ibid.*, pp. 51–53. See also p. 202.

79. *Ibid.*, p. 276. Also see pp. 277–92.

80. Leroy-Beaulieu, *De la colonisation chez les peuples modernes* (6th ed.), II, 626–27.

81. *Ibid.*, p. 627.

82. See, for example, Chailley-Bert, "La Politique indigène," *Revue économique internationale*, II (June 15–20, 1904), 50; and Valmor, *Les Problèmes de la colonisation*, pp. 51–56. Giran also had a few words on this subject: "Western education produces among peoples not prepared to receive it *déclassés*, dangerous individuals whom one can compare to our anarchists for whom a revolution alone can produce the opportunity to utilize their knowledge and satisfy their ambition." *De l'éducation des races*, p. 223.

83. Valmor, *Les Problèmes de la colonisation*, pp. 142–43.

84. Lavigne Sainte-Suzanne, "La Justice indigène aux colonies," *Questions diplomatiques et coloniales*, XVII (January 1, 1904), 26.

85. Le Bon, *Les Lois psychologiques de l'évolution des peuples* (6th ed.), p. 25.

86. Pacquier, "Sur l'âme noire," *Dépêche coloniale*, June 3, 1902.

87. Edmond Ferry, *La France en Afrique*, p. 228.

88. *Ibid.*, p. 232.

89. Clozel and Villaumin, *Les Coutumes indigènes de la Côte d'Ivoire*, p. 69.

90. *Ibid.*, p. 70.

91. Valmor, *Les Problèmes de la colonisation*, p. 145.

92. Speech given by Henri Lorin at the closing banquet of the Colonial Congress of 1904, *Rapport général du Congrès colonial français de 1904*, p. 106.

93. The problem of the *situation coloniale*, of contact between European and native, is studied in the introduction written by Mannoni to his *Psychologie de la colonisation*. A critical analysis of anthropological theory on this subject is Balandier, *Sociologie actuelle de l'Afrique noire*, Chapter 1.

94. See, for example, the views of Leroy-Beaulieu in "Le Budget et l'administration des colonies," *L'Economiste français*, II (December 3, 1904), 789–91.

95. Mille is best known for his *Barnavaux et quelques femmes;* Le Blond wrote *Le Zézère* and *Les Sortilèges*.

96. Mille, "La Race supérieure," *Revue de Paris*, I (February 15, 1905), 819–44.

97. Le Blond, "La Race inférieure," *Revue de Paris*, IV (July 1, 1906), 104–30.

98. Valmor was also concerned about the use of the idea of racial superiority as a justification for colonial expansion. *Les Problèmes de la colonisation*, p. 4.

99. Mille, "La Race supérieure," *Revue de Paris*, I (February 15, 1905), 820–21.

100. *Ibid.*, p. 821.   101. *Ibid.*, p. 830.

102. *Ibid.*, p. 844.

103. Le Blond, "La Race inférieure," *Revue de Paris*, IV (July 1, 1906), 106.

104. *Ibid.*, pp. 108–9.   105. *Ibid.*, p. 129.

106. *Ibid.*, p. 130.

Chapter 5. Imperialism: Expression of Man's Will to Power

1. On this subject, see the study by Nasmyth, *Social Progress and the Darwinian Theory*.

2. Gumplowicz, *Grundrise der Sociologie*, particularly pp. 114–17; and Vaccaro, *Bases sociologiques du Droit et de l'Etat*, trans. by Caure, pp. 79 ff.

3. On Novicow, see Worms, "Jacques Novicow," *Revue internationale de sociologie*, January, 1912, pp. 481–83.

4. Cited in Langer, *Diplomacy of Imperialism, 1890–1902*, I, 87.

5. Novicow, *Les Luttes entre sociétés humaines*, pp. 18–19.

6. Le Bon, *Les Premières civilisations*, p. 175.

7. *Ibid.*, p. 173.   8. *Ibid.*, p. 99.   9. *Ibid.*, p. 174.

10. The work appeared in four volumes: *Le Comte de Gobineau et l'aryanisme historique; Apollon ou Dionysos?; L'Impérialisme démocratique; Le Mal romantique.*

11. See *L'Impérialisme démocratique*, p. 16. Seillière referred to Helvétius as the "père légitime" of the idea of the will to power. He noted that the idea was expressed in Chapter XVII of *De l'Esprit* and more clearly present in Helvétius's work, *De l'Homme. Apollon ou Dionysos?*, p. 125.

12. See *L'Impérialisme démocratique*, pp. 4–5 and pp. 7–8.

13. *Apollon ou Dionysos?*, pp. xii–xiii.

14. *L'Impérialisme démocratique*, p. 8.

15. *Ibid.*, pp. 5–6 and p. 328.

16. Long a standard work on colonial legislation, Girault's *Principes de colonisation* went through many editions, the last of which appeared in 1942.

17. *Ibid.*, p. 29.   18. *Ibid.*   19. *Ibid.*, p. 31.

20. A recent treatment of the entire problem is Digeon, *La Crise allemande de la pensée française.*

21. The provocative book written by Prévost-Paradol in 1868, *La Nouvelle France*, contained the thought that France should settle on both sides of the Mediterranean in order to assure her greatness. Pp. 413–17.

22. Valmor, *Les Problèmes de la colonisation*, p. 3.

23. Vignon, "Les Colonies françaises," extract from the *Revue britannique*, reprinted in Paris, 1885, pp. 64–65.

24. Chailley-Bert, "La Politique coloniale de la France, ses procédés, ses résultats, et ses vues," *Indisch Genootschap*, April 10, 1899, p. 3.

25. See Deschamps, *Méthodes et doctrines coloniales de la France*, pp. 169–70.

26. Régismanset acknowledges use of this pseudonym in his *Questions coloniales, 1900–1912*, pp. 182–83.

27. Siger [Régismanset], *Essai sur la colonisation*, p. 17.

28. *Ibid.*, p. 18. 29. *Ibid.*, p. 57. 30. *Ibid.*, p. 62.

31. *Ibid.*, p. 68. 32. *Ibid.*, p. 70. 33. *Ibid.*, p. 92.

34. *Ibid.*, p. 106. The strong language used here by Régismanset was more tempered in *Questions coloniales*, when he declared that humanitarianism was the "reigning superstition," "a strange disease issued forth from the false idealism of 1789." P. 52.

35. *Essai sur la colonisation*, p. 57.

36. *Ibid.*, p. 118. 37. *Ibid.*, p. 119. 38. *Ibid.*, p. 120.

39. *Ibid.*, p. 131. 40. *Ibid.*, p. 126.

41. Siger [Régismanset], "Psychologie coloniale," *Mercure de France*, XXXVII (March, 1901), 795.

42. See *Questions coloniales*, pp. 182–83.

43. *Domination et colonisation*, p. 28. This idea of Harmand's was lauded by Georges Hardy, who wrote of it: "Nothing truer, it seems, than this principle which, reducing the colonial fact to the need for conservation and expansion of the human species, places it in the realm of the manifestations of the living world. It can serve as a point of departure for a philosophy of colonization." *La Politique coloniale et le partage de la terre*, p. 4.

44. *Domination et colonisation*, p. 29.

45. *Ibid.*, p. 30. 46. *Ibid.*, pp. 30–31.

47. *Ibid.*, p. 32. 48. See *ibid.*, pp. 33 ff.

49. *Ibid.*, p. 48. 50. *Ibid.*, p. 52.

51. *Ibid.*, p. 51. 52. *Ibid.*, pp. 52–53.

53. Harmand also believed that social fusion in Gaul was more sought by the conquered than the conqueror. *Ibid.*, p. 52.

54. *Ibid.* Cagnat in his *A travers le monde romain* makes a similar comparison, p. 293.

55. *Ibid.*, p. 152. 56. *Ibid.*, p. 153. 57. *Ibid.*

58. *Ibid.* 59. *Ibid.*, p. 154. 60. *Ibid.*, p. 155.

61. *Ibid.*

62. Lanessan, *Principes de colonisation,* p. 17.

63. Chailley-Bert, "La Politique coloniale en Allemagne," *Quinzaine coloniale* (April 10, 1909), p. 242.

64. Sarraut, *Grandeur et servitude coloniales,* p. 112.

Chapter 6. A New Policy: Association

1. A brief analysis of the development of this policy is to be found in Chailley-Bert, "La Politique de colonisation en Allemagne," *Quinzaine coloniale* (April 10, 1909). See also Roberts, *History of French Colonial Policy,* I, 110–15; and Knight, "French Colonial Policy—The Decline of 'Association,'" *Journal of Modern History,* V (June, 1933), 208–24.

2. See particularly Chailley-Bert, *Dix années de politique coloniale,* pp. 1–2. Etienne also condemned the so-called *bloc* theory; see his article, "Protectorat et décentralisation," *Dépêche coloniale,* December 29, 1902.

3. Harmand, *Domination et colonisation,* pp. 235–36.

4. Although Harmand employed the expression in his preface to the translation of Strachey's *India,* he had already suggested the idea in a lecture, "L'Indo-Chine française, politique et administration," which he gave in 1887 to the Association républicaine du centenaire de 1789.

5. Maunier, *Sociology of Colonies,* Vol. I, Chap. 28.

6. *Ibid.,* p. 297.

7. On their views, see *ibid.,* pp. 299–303.

8. See *ibid.,* p. 301, and for a general discussion of French opinion of the Quakers, see Phillips, *The Good Quaker in French Legend.*

9. Maunier, *Sociology of Colonies,* I, 300.

10. Bourdarie, "La Politique d'association," *Revue indigène* (January, 1906), p. 8.

11. See Brunschwig, *La Colonisation française,* pp. 170–76.

12. On Faidherbe, see Hardy, *Faidherbe.*

13. Cited in *ibid.,* p. 78.

14. Cited in *Gallieni au Tonkin, 1892–1896,* p. 227.

15. See *ibid.*, p. 233.

16. Gallieni, *Neuf ans à Madagascar*, p. 325.

17. Deschamps, *Gallieni Pacificateur*, p. 238.

18. *Ibid.*, pp. 240–41.   19. *Ibid.*, pp. 238–39.

20. Gallieni, *Neuf ans à Madagascar*, p. 325.

21. *Ibid.*, pp. 54–55.

22. "Instructions du 22 Mai 1898," in Deschamps, *Gallieni pacificateur*, p. 247.

23. One of the most favorable accounts of Gallieni's methods and their results in Madagascar was written by Ernest Lavisse. He stated: "It [Gallieni's method] allows the essential lines of the future edifice to be imagined. For the work of these thirty months appears to us to have been carried out according to a decided plan. It is one which, by the continuity of its views and the sureness of its principles, as by the flexibility of the means and the freedom allowed in its application, is not always encountered in our colonial undertakings." "Une méthode coloniale: l'armée et la colonisation," *Revue de Paris*, III (June 15, 1899), 682–83.

24. For a colorful account of the Lyautey family, see Maurois, *Lyautey*.

25. Lyautey's views on Gallieni's methods as applied in Indochina are expressed in his "Lettre du 5 février 1895 au Tonkin," in Hubert Lyautey, *Lettres du Tonkin et de Madagascar*, p. 113. Lyautey remarked to Gallieni: "I regard myself as the apostle of your ideas, the flagbearer of your method." Cited in *Gallieni au Tonkin*, p. 215.

26. "Lettre d'Anstatranan, le 24 mai 1897" in Hubert Lyautey, *Lettres du Tonkin et de Madagascar*, p. 539.

27. Hubert Lyautey, *Dans le sud de Madagascar*, p. 382.

28. "Allocution à Casablanca, le 29 juillet 1924," in Hubert Lyautey, *Paroles d'action*, pp. 411–12.

29. On Pennequin, see Brunschwig, *La Colonisation française*, pp. 182–83.

30. Lanessan, *L'Indo-Chine française*, p. 755.

31. Cited in Maunier, *Sociology of Colonies*, I, 297.

32. Harmand, *Domination et colonisation*, p. 159.

33. *Ibid.*, p. 164.   34. *Ibid.*, p. 161.   35. *Ibid.*, p. 163.
36. *Ibid.*, p. 170.   37. *Ibid.*, p. 160.
38. See Trouillet, "La Politique d'association," *Dépêche coloniale*, September 25, 1905.
39. See Harmand, *Domination et colonisation*, pp. 159–60. Bourdarie thought a policy of association was appropriate for Indochina but sought a policy of fusion in North Africa. See his "Au ministère des colonies," *Revue indigène*, March, 1911, pp. 129–34.
40. Joseph Caillaux emphasized this in a speech he made at the banquet held on June 8, 1905, for the French Colonial Congress of that year. See *Congrès colonial français de 1905*, p. 281.
41. Speech by Clémentel at the annual banquet of the Syndicat de la Presse coloniale française, cited in the *Dépêche coloniale*, January 5, 1906.
42. "Instructions du Ministre des Colonies au Gouverneur-général de l'Indo-Chine, Paris, le 28 décembre 1905," cited in the *Dépêche coloniale*, January 5, 1906. For favorable comments on this policy, see Pouvourville, "La Politique coloniale de M. Clémentel," *Dépêche coloniale*, January 5, 1906.
43. "Instructions du Ministre des Colonies au Gouverneur-général de l'Indo-Chine, Paris, le 28 décembre 1905," cited in *Dépêche coloniale*, January 5, 1906.
44. "Instructions du Ministre des Colonies au Gouverneur-général de Madagascar, Paris, le 28 décembre 1905," cited in *Dépêche coloniale*, January 5, 1906.
45. Caillaux, cited in *Congrès colonial français de 1905*, p. 281.
46. See particularly the address given by Lanessan, cited in the *Compte-rendu des travaux du Congrès colonial de Marseille*, I, 45.
47. Speech made by Marcel St. Germain at the opening session of the Colonial Congress of 1907, cited in *Congrès colonial français de 1907*, p. 49.
48. Speech cited *ibid.*, p. 98.
49. See the opinions of Roberts, *History of French Colonial Policy*, I, 121, and compare these with the critical appraisal of Knight, "French Colonial Policy—The Decline of 'Association,'" *Journal of Modern History*, V (June, 1933), 209.

50. Speech given at the monthly dinner of the Union coloniale française, October 19, 1905, cited in *Quinzaine coloniale* (October 25, 1905), p. 633. Lanessan spoke in a similar vein. See his speech cited in the *Compte-rendu des travaux du Congrès colonial de Marseille*, I, 37.

51. Ferry, "Préface" to Fauçon, *La Tunisie avant et depuis l'occupation française*, I, "b."

52. Pierre Lyautey, *L'Empire colonial français*, pp. 82–83. For Hanotaux's own statement about this incident, see "Discours de M. Gabriel Hanotaux," in Bremier *et al.*, *La Politique coloniale de la France*, p. 173.

53. Deschamps credits Gambetta with the remark in *Méthodes et doctrines coloniales de la France*, p. 134. Pierre Lyautey credits the remark to Barthélemy Saint-Hilaire in *L'Empire colonial français*, p. 130.

54. See the interpretation of Baron d'Estournelles de Constant in P. H. X. [Baron d'Estournelles de Constant], *La Politique française en Tunisie*, p. 320.

55. Cited in Deschamps, *Méthodes et doctrines coloniales de la France*, p. 135.

56. Chailley-Bert in *Indes orientales néerlandaises, Protectorat français en Asie et en Tunisie*, Vol. I of Bondewijnse and Chailley-Bert, *Le Régime des protectorats*, p. 154.

57. Hanotaux, "Le Traité de Tananarive," *Revue de Paris*, I (January 1, 1896), 10.

58. Chailley-Bert himself considered three types of protectorate: (1) *protectorat de gouvernement* (India offered numerous examples); (2) *protectorat de contrôle* (Cambodia was an example); (3) *protectorat d'administration* (Tonkin was an example). See *Indes orientales néerlandaises, Protectorat française en Asie et en Tunisie*, pp. 154–59.

59. See, for instance, Engelhardt, *Les Protectorats anciens et modernes;* and Gairal, *Le Protectorat international*.

60. Bodin, *Six Books of the Commonwealth*, trans. by Tooley, pp. 22–24.

61. See Pillet, *Des Droits de la puissance protectrice sur l'administration intérieure de l'Etat protégé*, pp. 2–3.

62. Brunel, *L'Etat et l'individu dans la colonisation française*

moderne, p. 37. August Billiard believed that the protectorate was not a permanent solution. Eventually, as French settled in the region, modification of laws and government would have to take place to accommodate them. As a result annexation would replace the protectorate. *Politique et organisation coloniales,* p. 28.

63. Gairal, *Le Protectorat international,* p. 270.

64. See Pillet, *Des Droits de la puissance protectrice,* p. 4.

65. Ferry, "Préface" to Fauçon, *La Tunisie avant et depuis l'occupation française,* I, "e"–"h."

66. Vignon, "La Politique du protectorat fondée sur l'inégalité des races," *Revue bleue,* III (April 1, 1905), 400.

67. Baréty, "La Politique indigène de la France," in Bremier et al., *La Politique coloniale de la France,* p. 76.

68. Cited in Fallex and Mairey, *La France et ses colonies au début du XXᵉ siècle,* p. 512.

69. See, for instance, the views of Messimy on association in Algeria in "Le Rapport de M. Messimy sur les petitions des indigènes algériens," *Quinzaine coloniale* (July 25, 1912), pp. 498–99.

70. See Deschamps, *Méthodes et doctrines coloniales de la France,* pp. 135–36.

71. Cited by Léal in "L'Oeuvre du protectorat et les interpellations sur la Tunisie," *Revue indigène* (March, 1912), p. 171. Speaking of Alapetite's speech, Léal commented: "These fine and sensible words simply signify that the policy of association . . . is officially recognized by the government." *Ibid.*

72. Cited by Bourdarie in "Au Maroc; conquête et colonisation," *Revue indigène* (August–September, 1912), p. 604.

73. See the critical remark of Deschamps, *Méthodes et doctrines coloniales de la France,* p. 150.

Chapter 7. *Economic Needs and the Policy of Association*

1. An appraisal of the problem of lack of French emigration to the colonies is found in J. B. Piolet, *La France hors de France.*

2. One writer, Louis Vignon, protested against this interpretation of economic necessity. Although he did believe in the importance of the colonies for the French economy, he did not imagine them in the role of markets as such. He believed that French goods were too expensive and too obviously destined for the luxury trade to find a market among the natives. It was the cheaper goods of England and Germany which would be purchased by the natives. Vignon did not believe that this fact reduced the value of overseas possessions for France. Such possessions were to be indirect markets. Raw materials coming from the colonial regions to France would be paid for by English mass-produced goods. Then the French would ship their luxury goods to England in order to eradicate the debt incurred with the English. See *L'Exploitation de notre empire colonial,* pp. 296–308.

3. Cited by Marchal in "La Pensée coloniale de la Révolution," *Congrès colonial française de 1904,* p. 24.

4. *De la colonisation chez les peuples modernes,* p. viii.

5. Mager, *Les Cahiers coloniaux de 1889,* p. iii.

6. Preface to *Tonkin et la Mère-Patrie,* cited in *Discours et opinions de Jules Ferry,* V, 558.

7. A not-so-typical interpretation of the acquisition of the French empire and its immediate economic value was contained in an anonymous article in the *Revue de Paris.* Arguing that the overseas possessions were not acquired with any clear economic purpose in mind, the author wrote: "There was no one in France who understood exactly the advantages France could obtain from these new possessions. . . . In reality we found ourselves embarrassed by territories which we did not know what to do with, whose populations and resources were equally unknown to us." "L'Effort colonial," *Revue de Paris,* V (September 15, 1902), 425.

8. On this subject, see the comments of Roberts, *History of French Colonial Policy,* II, 634.

9. See Feis, *Europe, the World's Banker 1870–1914,* pp. 51-55.

10. Aron, "The Leninist Myth of Imperialism," *Partisan Review,* XVII (November–December, 1951), 647.

11. Bleton, *Les Hommes du temps qui viennent*, p. 217.

12. See Brunschwig, "Le Parti colonial français," *Revue française d'histoire d'outre-mer*, XLVI (1959), 83. It would appear that this theme is expounded in Brunschwig's most recent volume, *Mythes et réalités de l'impérialisme colonial français, 1871–1914* (Paris, Colin, 1960), which appeared after completion of this study.

13. Etienne, "Les Compagnies de colonisation," cited in *Eugène Etienne*, I, 22.

14. *Débats parlementaires, Chambre des Députés, Journal officiel*, December 1, 1891, p. 2381.

15. Speech made in the Chamber of Deputies, March 6, 1899, cited in *Eugène Etienne*, I, 291.

16. Etienne, "Un Programme de politique coloniale," *Questions diplomatiques et coloniales*, XI (January 15, 1901), 72–73.

17. A letter from Etienne to the French Colonial Congress printed in *Rapport général du Congrès colonial français de 1904*, p. iv.

18. Saint-Germain, "Rapport sur le budget des colonies," cited in *Dépêche coloniale*, April 6, 1906.

19. Examples of this opinion are to be found in Vignon, *L'Exploitation de notre empire colonial*, p. 6 and p. 216; Aubrey, *La Colonisation et les colonies*, pp. 110–11; and Lorin, *La France puissance coloniale*, pp. 91–92 and p. 467.

20. Lanessan, *Principes de colonisation*, p. 31.

21. At the Colonial Congress of Marseille he stated that something other than assimilation had been needed in colonial administration. "This other thing was the policy of the protectorate to which I and others had given the name of policy of association." *Compte-rendu des travaux du Congrès colonial de Marseille*, I, 37.

22. Lanessan, *Principes de colonisation*, pp. 86–87.

23. *Ibid.*, p. 86.   24. *Ibid.*, pp. 150–51.

25. *Ibid.*, p. 241.

26. Billiard, *Politiques et organisations coloniales*, pp. 8–9.

27. *Ibid.*, p. 9.   28. *Ibid.*, p. 45.

29. *Ibid.*, p. 16.   30. *Ibid.*, p. 24.

31. *Ibid.*, pp. 23–24 and p. 27.

32. In Billiard's opinion the best example of the state meeting all the demands of the protectorate regime was Tunisia. *Ibid.*, p. 27.

33. *Ibid.*, p. 28. 34. *Ibid.*, pp. 274–75.

35. *Ibid.*, p. 280. 36. *Ibid.*, p. 26.

37. Etienne wrote: "We are not philosophers; we are men of action. . . . We want our colonies to strengthen, extend and enrich France; we must act and act practically. . . ." *Rapport général du Congrès colonial français de 1904*, p. iv.

38. *Rapport général des séances des sections, Congrès colonial français de 1904*, pp. 4–5.

39. On Pouvourville, see Chapter 8.

40. Pouvourville, "La Main d'oeuvre des colonies," *Rapports présentés à la VIᵉ Section, Congrès colonial français de 1904*, p. 2.

41. *Ibid.* 42. *Ibid.*, p. 5.

43. Valmor, *Les Problèmes de la colonisation*, pp. 137–63.

44. *Ibid.*, p. 75. 45. *Ibid.*, pp. 78–79.

46. *Ibid.*, pp. 81–85.

47. *Ibid.*, p. 88. Giran also insisted that the natives must be taught the "taste for work." *De l'éducation des races*, pp. 297–98.

48. Valmor, *Les Problèmes de la colonisation*, p. 59.

49. *Domination et colonisation*, p. 9.

50. *Ibid.*, p. 11.

51. See Sarraut, *La Mise en valeur des colonies françaises*.

52. *Domination et colonisation*, p. 12.

53. *Ibid.*, p. 133. 54. *Ibid.*, p. 150.

55. *Ibid.*, pp. 150–51. 56. *Ibid.*, p. 158.

57. *Ibid.*

58. His small volume, *Dix Années de politique coloniale*, contains his most salient ideas.

59. A good example is *Le Rôle social de la colonisation*.

60. See *La Colonisation française au XIXᵉ siècle*, p. 24 and pp. 96–97.

61. *Où en est la politique coloniale de la France: l'âge de l'agriculture*, p. 20. Also see "Les Idées en marche; le progrès

colonial," *Quinzaine coloniale* (November 25, 1898), p. 673. On Chailley-Bert's explanations for the poor results of France's agricultural program in the colonies, see "La Colonisation agricole dans les colonies françaises," *Quinzaine coloniale* (October 25, 1903), pp. 673–75.

62. *Où en est la politique coloniale de la France*, p. 20. Vignon agreed with Chailley-Bert's ideas concerning the "age of agriculture." See his *L'Exploitation de notre empire colonial*, p. 55.

63. *Où en est la politique coloniale de la France*, p. 20.

64. See *La Colonisation française au XIXᵉ siècle*, pp. 19–20.

65. *Où en est la politique coloniale de la France*, pp. 9–10

66. "La France et la Plus Grande France," Extract from the *Revue politique et parlementaire* (August, 1902), p. 5. See also "La Politique coloniale et ses résultats," *Quinzaine coloniale* (October 25, 1908), pp. 899–900; and *Dix années de politique coloniale*, pp. 35–36 and pp. 104–6.

67. *Dix années de politique coloniale*, pp. 43–44.

68. *Ibid.*, pp. 1–2.   69. *Ibid.*, p. 6.   70. *Ibid.*, p. 11.

71. "Le Besoin des méthodes en administration coloniale," *Quinzaine coloniale* (February 25, 1902), p. 99.

72. "L'Agriculture aux colonies," *Quinzaine coloniale* (March 10, 1904), p. 147.

73. "La Politique indigène," *Revue économique internationale*, II (June 15–20, 1904), 44.

74. *Ibid.*, pp. 44–45.   75. *Ibid.*, p. 45.   76. *Ibid.*

77. *Ibid.*, p. 49.   78. *Ibid.*, p. 50.   79. *Ibid.*, p. 57.

80. "La Politique coloniale en Allemagne," *Quinzaine coloniale* (April 10, 1909), p. 242.

81. "La Politique coloniale de la France," *Quinzaine coloniale* (August 10, 1903), p. 515.

Chapter 8. Military Problems and the Policy of Association

1. Cited in Ferradini, *Essai sur la défense des colonies*, p. 24. Etienne believed that this expression might have held true in former days but that Fashoda had totally changed the situation.

The "center of gravity of European peace is no longer exclusively in the quarrels of Europe. . . ." "La Défense des colonies," *Dépêche coloniale*, June 15–16, 1902.

2. On the organization of the colonial army, see *L'Armée coloniale, lois, décrets, circulaires concernant son organisation.*

3. Ferradini, *Essai sur la défense des colonies*, p. 114.

4. See the opinions of Pouvourville expressed during the French Colonial Congress of 1906, "XVIIᵉ Section, Organisation militaire," *Congrès colonial français de 1906*, p. 310.

5. Gain, *L'Armée coloniale et la défense des colonies*, p. 2; and Etienne, "La Défense des colonies," *Dépêche coloniale*, June 15–16, 1902.

6. Bourdarie, "La Politique d'association," *Revue indigène*, January, 1906, p. 2.

7. Cited in Sarraut, *La Mise en valeur des colonies françaises*, p. 93.

8. *Compte-rendu des travaux du Congrès colonial de Marseille*, I, 62.

9. *Ibid.*, p. 66.

10. Bourdarie, "La Politique d'association," *Revue indigène* (January, 1906), p. 8.

11. On French opinion concerning this subject see "La Guerre russo-japonaise, causes et conséquences," *Dépêche coloniale*, January 27, 1906.

12. See "Le Péril jaune, un document sensationnel," *Echo de Paris*, January 10, 11, 12, 1905. The validity of this report was attested to by the editors of the *Echo de Paris* who stated that they had obtained a copy of it in English from a British embassy in a "Far Eastern country." In *Le Temps* of January 11, 1905, M. Motono, Japanese ambassador to France, denied the authenticity of the report. True or not, the document aroused considerable excitement in French colonial circles. The fact that Baron Kodama was chief of staff of the Japanese field armies in 1905 only caused more concern.

13. "Le Rapport Kodama," *Echo de Paris*, January 10, 1905.

14. *Ibid.*, January 11, 1905.

15. See Pouvourville, "Le Rapport Kodama et la défense de

l'Indo-Chine," *Dépêche coloniale*, January 31, 1905; and "Sur le programme de défense de l'Indo-Chine," *Dépêche coloniale*, October 9, 1905.

16. Lorin, "A propos du péril jaune," *Dépêche coloniale*, February 1, 1905.

17. "La Domination européenne et ses chances d'avenir en Extrême-Orient," *Revue britannique*, VI (1900), 56.

18. See the speech of Captain d'Ollone at the monthly dinner of the Union coloniale française, cited in the *Dépêche coloniale*, February 11, 1905.

19. See "La Défense de l'Indo-Chine, rapport Deloncle," *Dépêche coloniale*, May 10, 1905.

20. Lorin, "La Sécurité de l'Indo-Chine," *Dépêche coloniale*, March 28, 1905.

21. Speech of Clémentel to the annual banquet of the Syndicat de la Presse coloniale française, cited in the *Dépêche coloniale*, March 28, 1905.

22. His novel, *Annam sanglant*, contributed to the growth of interest in exotic literature in France, and his works written under the pseudonym "Matgiori" were designed to compare Western philosophy with Eastern metaphysics.

23. Pouvourville, *Les Défenses de l'Indo-Chine et la politique d'association*, p. 29.

24. He also analyzed this problem during the French Colonial Congress of 1905. See "Comment et avec qui nous défendrons l'Indo-Chine," *Congrès colonial français de 1905*, pp. 25 ff.

25. *Les Défenses de l'Indo-Chine et la polititque d'association*, pp. 112–13.

26. *Ibid.*, p. 88.

27. Pouvourville had definite opinions about the policy of the protectorate and that of assimilation in Indochina. The protectorate was discarded because it rested on a fallacious idea. "It supposes . . . without the slightest exception possible the inferiority of the protected people." The error of assimilation was of an opposite extreme: belief in the equality of native and European. In practice, Pouvourville added, such a policy was

but a part of the "realm of speculative curiosities." *Ibid.*, pp. 127–32.

28. *Ibid.*, p. 139.   29. *Ibid.*
30. *Ibid.*, p. 140.   31. *Ibid.*, p. 156.
32. *Ibid.*, pp. 159–90.   33. *Ibid.*, p. 194.
34. *Ibid.*, p. 222.

35. "Comment et avec qui nous défendrons l'Indo-Chine," *Congrès colonial français de 1905*, p. 27.

36. Pouvourville, "Le Maître de l'indigène," *Dépêche coloniale*, November 21, 1906.

37. Cited in Brunschwig, *Histoire de la colonisation française*, pp. 276–77.

38. Trouillet, "Politique d'association," *Dépêche coloniale*, September 25, 1905.

39. See the speech of Paul Bodin at the French Colonial Congress of 1906, cited in *Congrès colonial français de 1906*, p. 82.

Chapter 9. Ideal and Reality

1. See the preface of Sarraut's *Mise en valeur des colonies françaises*, particularly p. 19.

2. Trabant, "Association, assimilation, adaptation," *Dépêche coloniale*, September 21, 1908.

3. Siger [Régismanset], *Essai sur la colonisation*, p. 125.

4. Harmand, *Domination et colonisation*, p. 159.

5. *Ibid.*, p. 170.   6. See Chapter 4.

7. Saussure, "Comment assimiler l'indigène," "Rapports présentés à la Ve section," *Congrès colonial français de 1904*, p. 7.

8. *Ibid.*, p. 18.   9. *Ibid.*

10. See, for instance, Valmor, *Les Problèmes de la colonisation*, p. 133.

11. Speech made at the banquet of June 8, 1905, French Colonial Congress of 1905, *Congrès colonial français de 1905*, p. 279.

12. *Recueil du Congrès colonial national*, pp. 18–19.

13. The similarity between the intentions of the "association-ists" and the "assimilators" was insisted upon by Louis Vignon: "The secret opinions of the 'associationists' are always close to the avowed ones of the 'assimilators.'" *Un Programme de politique coloniale*, p. 202.

14. Wrote the Dutch author Kat Angelino of French as-similation: "As a matter of fact this policy, which at the outset met with much appreciation and even enthusiasm on the part of the colonial population, formed an almost unavoidable stage of transition from the system of exploitation to modern colonial policy." *Colonial Policy*, trans. by Renier, I, 11.

15. The famous Macaulay Education Act of 1833 need only be recalled.

16. Mille, "La Race supérieure," *Revue de Paris*, I (February 15, 1905), 821.

17. See Brunschwig, *La Colonisation française*, p. 187.

18. Mus, *Destin de l'Union française*, p. 293.

19. Deschamps, *Méthodes et doctrines coloniales de la France*, pp. 213–14.

20. Knight, "French Colonial Policy—The Decline of 'As-sociation,'" *Journal of Modern History*, V (June, 1933), 217.

21. Eboué conceived of a *Statut des notables évolués* in which the notables "would thus become actual citizens of the colony and as such would be called upon to demonstrate their ability in the administration of their own commune under our con-trol." Cited in Deschamps, *Méthodes et doctrines coloniales de la France*, p. 178.

22. Léal, "L'Oeuvre du protectorat et les interpellations sur la Tunisie," *Revue indigène* (March, 1912), p. 172.

23. Messimy in "Le Rapport de M. Messimy sur les petitions des indigènes algériens," *Quinzaine coloniale*, July 25, 1912, p. 499.

24. Peyrat, "Le Cas de l'élite indigène dans l'Afrique du Nord," *Revue indigène* (February, 1912), p. 81.

BIBLIOGRAPHY

Armée coloniale, lois, décrets, circulaires concernant son organisation. Paris: Charles-Lavauzelle, 1900.

Arnaud, A., and H. Méray. *Les Colonies françaises, organisation administrative, judicaire, politique et financière.* Paris: Augustin Challamel, 1900.

Aron, Raymond. "The Leninist Myth of Imperialism," *Partisan Review*, XVIII (November-December, 1951), 646–62.

Aubin, Eugène. *Les Anglais aux Indes et en Egypte.* Paris: A. Colin, 1909.

Aubrey, Pierre. *La Colonisation et les colonies.* Paris: O. Doin et fils, 1909.

Baillaud, Emile. *La Politique indigène de l'Angleterre en Afrique occidentale.* Paris: Hachette, 1913.

Balandier, Georges. *Sociologie actuelle de l'Afrique noire: Dynamique des changements sociaux en Afrique centrale.* Paris: Presses universitaires de France, 1955.

Bardoux, Jacques. *L'Angleterre radicale: Essai de psychologie social, 1906–1913.* Paris: Félix Alcan, 1913.

Baréty, Léon. "La Politique indigène de la France," in Bremier et al. *La Politique coloniale de la France.* Paris: Félix Alcan, 1924.

Bérard, Victor. *L'Angleterre et l'impérialisme.* Paris: A. Colin, 1900.

Bibesco, Princess. *Images d'Epinal.* Paris: Librairie Plon, 1937.

Billiard, Auguste. *Politique et organisation coloniales.* Paris: Girard et Brière, 1899.

Blet, Henri. *France d'Outre-Mer.* Vol. III: *L'Oeuvre coloniale de la Troisième République.* Grenoble: Arthaud, 1950.

Bleton, Pierre. *Les Hommes du temps qui viennent.* Paris: Les Editions ouvrières, économiques et humanistes, 1956.

Blois, Jules. "Les Anglais dans l'Inde," *Revue bleue,* XIX (April 11, 1903), 476–80.

Bodin, Jean. *Six Books of the Commonwealth.* Trans. by M. J. Tooley. Oxford: Basil Blackwell, n.d.

Bondewijnse, J. See Chailley-Bert, Joseph, *Le Régime des protectorats.*

Bonvalot, Gabriel. "L'Administration coloniale anglaise," *Revue bleue,* IX (June 11, 1898), 758–61.

Bourdarie, Paul. "Au Maroc: conquête et colonisation," *Revue indigène* (August-September, 1912), pp. 602–11.

—— "Au Ministère des colonies," *Revue indigène* (March, 1911), pp. 129–34.

—— "La Politique d'association," *Revue indigène* (January, 1906), pp. 11–21.

Boutmy, Emile. *Essai d'une psychologie politique du peuple anglais au XIXᵉ siècle.* Paris: A. Colin, 1901.

Brunel, Louis. *L'Etat et l'individu dans la colonisation française moderne.* Paris: A. Fontemoing, 1898.

Brunschwig, Henri. *La Colonisation française.* Paris: Calmann-Levy, 1949.

—— "Le Parti colonial français," *Revue française d'histoire d'outre-mer,* XLVI (1959), 49–83.

Caboton, A. *Les Indes néerlandaises.* Paris: A. Guilmoto, 1910.

Cagnat, R. *A travers le monde romain.* 2d. ed. Paris: Fontemoing et Cie., 1912.

Castre, Charles. *The Ideals of France.* New York: The Abingdon Press, 1922.

Chailley-Bert, Joseph. "L'Agriculture aux colonies," *Quinzaine coloniale* (March 10, 1904).

—— "Le Besoin des méthodes en administration coloniale," *Quinzaine coloniale* (February 25, 1902).

—— *La Colonisation de l'Indo-Chine; l'expérience anglaise.* Paris: A. Colin, 1892.

—— *La Colonisation française au XIXᵉ siècle.* Paris: Union coloniale française, 1896.

—— *Dix années de politique coloniale.* Paris: Armand Colin, 1902.

—— "Les Enseignements de Fachoda," *Quinzaine coloniale* (November 10, 1898).

—— "La Forme des colonies et son influence sur la législation qui leur convient," *L'Economiste français*, II (February 27, 1892), 262–64.

—— "La France et la Plus Grande France." Extract from the *Revue politique et parlementaire*, August, 1902.

—— *La Hollande et les fonctionnaires des Indes néerlandaises.* Paris: A. Colin, 1902.

—— "Les Idées en marche; le progrès colonial," *Quinzaine coloniale* (November 25, 1898).

—— *Java et ses habitants.* Paris: A. Colin, 1900.

—— *Où en est la politique coloniale de la France: l'âge de l'agriculture.* Paris: A. Colin, 1896.

—— "La Politique coloniale de la France," *Quinzaine coloniale* (August 10, 1903).

—— "La Politique coloniale de la France, ses procédés, ses résultats et ses vues," *Indisch Genootschap* (April 10, 1899).

—— "La Politique coloniale en Allemagne," *Quinzaine coloniale* (April 10, 1909).

—— "La Politique coloniale et ses résultats," *Quinzaine coloniale* (October 25, 1908).

—— "La Politique indigène," *Revue économique internationale*, II (June 15–20, 1904).

—— and J. Bondewijnse. *Le Régime des protectorats.* 2 vols. Brussels: Institut international colonial, 1899.

—— *Le Rôle social de la colonisation.* Paris: Siège du Comité de défense et de progrès social, 1897.

Chatenet, P. "The Civil Service in France," in William A. Robson, ed., *The Civil Service in Britain and France.* London: The Hogarth Press, 1956.

Clough, Shepard B. *France, a History of National Economics: 1789–1939.* New York: Charles Scribner's Sons, 1939.

Clozel, F. J., and Robert Villaumin. *Les Coutumes indigènes de la Côte d'Ivoire.* Paris: A. Challamel, 1902.

Compte-rendu des travaux du Congrès colonial de Marseille, 1906. 2 vols. Paris: Guillaumin et Cie., 1908.

Compte-rendu du Congrès international de Paris, 1889. Paris: A. Challamel, 1889.

Congrès colonial français. 1903–8. Paris: Imprimerie spéciale des Congrès coloniaux français.

Congrès des anciennes colonies, Paris, 1909. Coulomniers: Imprimerie Dessaint et Cie., 1909.

Congrès international colonial: Rapports, mémoires et procès-verbaux des séances, Paris, 1900. Paris: Exposition universelle internationale de 1900, 1901.

Congrès international de sociologie coloniale. 2 vols. Paris: Armand Colin, 1901.

Cultru, P. "Esprit de la politique indigène de l'Angleterre en Afrique occidentale," *Quinzaine coloniale* (February 10, 1914).

Cureau, A. *Les Sociétés primitives de l'Afrique équitoriale.* Paris: F. Alcan, 1912.

Davray, Henry-D. "L'Angleterre et la préponderance européenne," *Mercure de France,* XXXVIII (June, 1901), 659–70.

Delavignette, Robert, and Charles-André Julien. *Les Constructeurs de la France d'Outre-Mer.* Paris: Editions Correa, 1946.

Demangeon, A. "La Politique coloniale," in Augé-Laribé *et al., La Politique républicaine.* 2d ed. Paris: Félix Alcan, 1924.

Démaret, Emile. *Organisation coloniale et fédération, une fédération de la France et de ses colonies.* Paris: Imprimerie de Charles Roblet, 1899.

Démolins, Edmond. *A quoi tient la supériorité des Anglo-Saxons?* 11th ed. Paris: Librairie de Paris, 1899. Translated as *Anglo-Saxon Superiority.* London: The Leadenhall Press, 1898.

Denancy, Edgard. *Philosophie de la colonisation.* Paris. Bibliothèque de "La Critique," 1902.

Deschamps, Hubert, Ed. *Gallieni pacificateur.* Paris: Presses universitaires de France, 1949.

—— *Méthodes et doctrines coloniales de la France.* Paris: A. Colin, 1953.

Dilke, Sir Charles. *Greater Britain, a Record of Travel in English-Speaking Countries during 1866 and 1867.* London: Macmillan and Co., 1868.

Dubois, Marcel, and Auguste Terrier. *Un Siècle d'expansion coloniale.* Paris: Librairie maritime et coloniale, 1902.

Durand, A. *Notre nouvelle politique coloniale.* Paris: Librairie africaine et coloniale, 1906.

Durkheim, Emile. *Règles de la méthode sociologique.* Paris: Félix Alcan, 1895.

"L'Effort colonial," *Revue de Paris*, V (September 15, 1902), 422–48.

Engelhardt, Edouard. *Les Protectorats anciens et modernes.* Paris: A. Pédone, 1896.

Estournelles de Constant, Baron d'. *See* P. H. X.

Etienne, Eugène. "La Défenses des colonies," *Dépêche coloniale* (June 15–16, 1902).

—— *Eugène Etienne, son oeuvre coloniale, algérienne et politique, 1881–1906.* 2 vols. Paris: Flammarion, 1907.

—— "Un Programme de politique coloniale," *Questions diplomatiques et coloniales*, XI (January 15, 1901), 65–82.

—— "Protectorat et décentralisation," *Dépêche coloniale* (December 28, 1902).

Eutrope, E. *Le Régime politique des colonies anglaises à self-government.* Paris: Recueil Sirey, 1908.

Fallex, M., and A. Mairey. *La France et ses colonies au début du XXe siècle.* Paris: Charles Delagrave, n.d.

Fallot, E. *L'Avenir colonial de la France.* Paris: Delagrave, 1902.

Feis, Herbert. *Europe the World's Banker: An Account of European Foreign Investment and the Connection of World Finance with Diplomacy Before the War.* New Haven: Yale University, 1930.

Ferrandini, Captain. *Essai sur la défense des colonies.* Paris: Charles-Lavauzelle, 1903.

Ferry, Edmond. *La France en Afrique.* Paris: Armand Colin, 1905.

Ferry, Jules. *Discours et opinions de Jules Ferry.* 5 vols. Paris: Armand Colin, 1895–98.

—— "Préface" to Narcisse Fauçon, *La Tunisie avant et depuis l'occupation française*. 2 vols. Paris: Challamel, 1893.

Fouillée, Alfred. "Le Caractère des races humaines et l'avenir de la race blanche," *Revue des deux mondes*, CXXIV (July 1, 1894), 76–107.

—— *Education from a National Standpoint*. Trans. and ed. by W. J. Greenstreet. New York: D. Appleton and Co., 1892.

—— *Esquisse psychologique des peuples européens*. Paris: Félix Alcan, 1903.

—— *et al. Modern French Legal Philosophy*. Trans. by Mrs. Franklin W. Scott and Joseph P. Chamberlain. Vol. VII of the *Modern Legal Philosophy Series*. Boston: The Boston Book Company, 1916.

—— "La Psychologie des peuples et l'anthropologie," *Revue des deux mondes*, CXXVIII (March 15, 1895), 365–96.

—— *Psychologie du peuple français* 6th ed. Paris: Félix Alcan, 1914.

Furnival, John S. *Colonial Policy and Practice, a Comparative Study of Burma and the Netherlands India*. Cambridge: Cambridge University Press, 1948.

Gaffarel, Paul. *La Politique coloniale en France de 1789 à 1830*. Paris: Félix Alcan, 1908.

Gain, Edmond. *L'Armée coloniale et la défense des colonies*. Paris: Société de l'Annuaire coloniale, 1904.

Gairal, François. *Le Protectorat international*. Paris: A. Pédone, n.d.

Gallieni, Joseph. *Gallieni au Tonkin, 1892–1896*. Paris: Editions Berger-Levrault, 1941.

—— *Neuf ans à Madagascar*. Paris: Hachette, 1908.

Gannay, Paul. *L'Impérialisme économique et la grande industrie anglaise*. Paris: Librairie générale de Droit et de Jurisprudence, 1905.

Garrett, Mitchell B. *The French Colonial Question, 1789–1791*. Ann Arbor: George Wehr, 1918.

Giran, Paul. *De l'éducation des races*. Paris: Augustin Challamel, 1913.

Girault, Arthur. *The Colonial Tariff Policy of France*. Oxford: Clarendon Press, 1916.

—— *Principes de colonisation et de législation coloniale*. 1st ed. Paris: Recueil Sirey, 1895.

Gobineau, Joseph Arthur de. *Essai sur l'inégalité des races humaines*. 4 vols. Paris: Firmin Didot Frères, 1853–55.

Gonnaud, A. *La Colonisation hollandaise à Java*. Paris: A. Challamel, 1905.

Greswell, William P. *The Growth and Administration of the British Colonies, 1837–1897*. London: Blackie and Son, 1898.

Gumplowicz, Ludwig. *Grundrise des Sociologie*. Vienna: Manz'sche k.k. Hof-Verlangs-und Universitats-Buchhandlung, 1885.

Guyot, Yves. *Lettres sur la politique coloniale*. Paris: C. Reinwald, 1885.

Hanotaux, Gabriel. *L'Energie française*. Paris: Flammarion, 1902.

—— "Le Traité de Tananarive," *Revue de Paris*, I (January 1, 1896), 681–98.

Hardy, Georges. *Faidherbe*. Paris: Editions de l'Encyclopédie de l'empire français, 1947.

—— *Histoire de la colonisation française*. 5th ed. Paris: Larose, 1947.

—— *Histoire sociale de la colonisation française*. Paris: Larose, 1953.

—— *La Politique coloniale et le partage de la terre*. Paris: Editions Albin Michel, 1937.

Harmand, Jules. *Domination et colonisation*. Paris: Ernest Flammarion, 1910.

Helvétius, Claude Adrien. *Oeuvres complètes de M. Helvétius*. 5 vols. London, 1781.

Henry, René. "Sommes-nous des Latins?" *Questions diplomatiques et coloniales*, XVII (May 1, 1904), 657–63.

Hobson, J. A. *Imperialism: a Study*. 3d ed. London: George Allen and Unwin, 1954.

Howe, Suzanne. *Novels of Empire*. New York: Columbia University Press, 1949.

Humbert, Charles. *L'Oeuvre française aux colonies.* Paris: E. Larose, 1913.

James, Henry. *Parisian Sketches, Letters to the New York Herald, 1875–1876.* Leon Edel and Ilse Lind, eds. New York: New York University Press, 1957.

Journal Officiel de la République française.

Julien, Charles-André. *Les Politiques coloniales.* Paris: Cours de Droit, 1947.

—— ed. *Les Techniciens de la colonisation: XIXᵉ–XXᵉ siècles.* Vol. I of *Première Série, Etudes coloniales: Colonies et empires.* C.-A. Julien, ed. Paris: Presses universitaires de France, 1947.

—— *See* Delavignette, Robert.

Kat Angelino, A. D. A. de. *Colonial Policy.* Trans. by G. J. Renier. 2 vols. Chicago: University of Chicago Press, 1931.

Knight, M. M. "French Colonial Policy—The Decline of 'Association,'" *Journal of Modern History,* V (June, 1933), 208–24.

Lahy, J. M. "La Colonisation scientifique," *Dépêche coloniale* (February 1, 1907).

Lamartine, Alphonse de. *Voyage en Orient.* Paris: Hachette, 1875.

Lampué, P. *See* Rolland, L.

Lanessan, Jean-L. de. *L'Indo-Chine française; étude politique, économique et administrative sur la Cochinchine, le Cambodge, L'Annam et le Tonkin.* Paris: Félix Alcan, 1889.

—— *Principes de colonisation.* Paris: Félix Alcan, 1897.

Langer, William L. *The Diplomacy of Imperialism, 1890–1902.* 2 vols. New York: Alfred A. Knopf, 1935.

Lavergne, Bernard. *Une Révolution dans la politique coloniale de la France, le problème de l'Afrique du Nord.* Paris: Editions Librairie Mercure, 1948.

Lavigne, Sainte-Suzanne, L. J. "La Justice indigène aux colonies," *Questions diplomatiques et coloniales,* XVII (January 1, 1904), 24–29.

Lavisse, Ernest. "Une Méthode coloniale: l'armée et la colonisation," *Revue de Paris,* III (June 15, 1899), 681–98.

Léal, Numa. "L'Oeuvre du Protectorat et les interpellations sur la Tunisie," *Revue indigène* (March, 1912), pp. 168–79.

Le Blond, Marius-Ary. "La Race inférieure," *Revue de Paris*, IV (July 1, 1906), 104–30.

Le Bon, Gustave. *L'Homme et les sociétés, leurs origines et leur histoire.* 2 vols. Paris: J. Rothschild, 1881.

—— *Les Lois psychologiques de l'évolution des peuples.* 1st ed. Paris: Félix Alcan, 1894. 6th ed. Paris: Félix Alcan, 1906.

—— *Les Premières civilisations.* Paris: C. Marzon and E. Flammarion, 1889.

Leclerc, Max. *L'Education des classes moyennes et dirigéantes en Angleterre.* Paris: A. Colin, 1894.

Leclerq, Jules. "Java et le système colonial des Hollandais," *Revue des deux mondes*, CXLIV (November 1, 1897), 161–87.

Lemire, Charles. *Le Peuplement de nos colonies.* Paris: A. Challamel, 1900.

Leroy-Beaulieu, Pierre-Paul. "Le Budget et l'administration des colonies," *L'Economiste français*, II (December 3, 1904), 789–91.

—— "Les Colonies anglaises et les projets d'organisation de l'Empire britannique," *Revue des deux mondes*, CXXXIX (January 1, 1907), 121–59.

—— *De la colonisation chez les peuples modernes.* 2d ed. Paris: Guillaumin et Cie., 1882. 6th ed., 2 vols. Paris: Guillaumin, 1906.

—— "Les Principes du régime des indigènes dans les colonies," *L'Economiste français*, II (December 2, 1899), 785–88.

—— "Le Problème colonial aux Etats-Unis," *L'Economiste français*, II (December 3, 1898), 751–53.

Lévy-Bruhl, Lucien. *Les Carnets de Lévy-Bruhl.* Paris: Presses universitaires de France, 1949.

—— *Les Fonctions mentales dans les sociétés inférieures.* Paris: Félix Alcan, 1900.

Lokke, Carl L. *France and the Colonial Question: a Study of Contemporary French Opinion, 1763–1801.* New York: Columbia University Press, 1932.

Lorin, Henri. "A propos de péril jaune," *Dépêche colonial* (February 1, 1905).

—— *La France puissance coloniale*. Paris: A. Challamel, 1906.

—— "Les Hollandais et la politique d'association," *Dépêche coloniale* (October 24, 1905).

Lyautey, Hubert. *Dans le Sud de Madagascar*. Paris: H. Charles Lavauzelle, 1903.

—— *Du rôle colonial de l'armée*. Paris: Armand Colin, 1900.

—— *Lettres du Tonkin et de Madagascar*. Paris: A. Colin, 1921.

—— *Paroles d'action*. Paris: Armand Colin, 1927.

Lyautey, Pierre. *L'Empire colonial français*. Paris: Les Editions de France, 1931.

Mager, Henri. *Les Cahiers coloniaux de 1889*. Paris: A. Colin, 1889.

Mairey, A. *See* Fallex, M.

Mannoni, O. *Psychologie de la colonisation*. Paris: Editions du Seuil, 1950.

Maunier, René. *The Sociology of Colonies*. Ed. and trans. by E. O. Lorimer. 2 vols. London: Routledge and Kegan Paul, 1949.

Maurois, André. *Lyautey*. Paris: Plon, 1931.

McKay, Donald. "Colonialism in the French Geographical Movement, 1871–1881," *Geographical Review*, XXXIII (1943), 214–32.

Méray, H. *See* Arnaud, A.

Messimy, A. *Notre Oeuvre coloniale*. Paris: E. Larose, 1910.

Meynier, Octave. *L'Afrique noire*. Paris: Flammarion, 1911.

Michelet, Jules. *Le Peuple*. Paris: Librairie Marcel Didier, 1946.

Mille, Pierre. "La Race supérieure," *Revue de Paris*, I (February 15, 1905), 819–44.

Moon, Parker T. *Imperialism and World Politics*. New York: The Macmillan Co., 1926.

Mornet, Daniel. *Les Origines intellectuelles de la Révolution française*. 5th ed. Paris: A. Colin, 1953.

—— *La Pensée française au XVIIIᵉ siècle*. 2d ed. Paris: Armand Colin, 1929.

Murphy, Agnes. *The Ideology of French Imperialism*. Washington: Catholic University Press, 1948.

Mus, Paul. *Le Destin de l'Union française: De l'Indo-Chine à Afrique.* Paris: Editions du Seuil, 1954.

Nasmyth, George. *Social Progress and the Darwinian Theory.* New York: G. P. Putnam's Sons, 1916.

Novicow, Jacques. *Les Luttes entre sociétés humaines et leurs phases successives.* Paris: Félix Alcan, 1893.

Orléans, Prince Henri. *Politique extérieure et coloniale.* Paris: Ernest Flammarion, n.d.

Pacquier, Léon. "Sur l'âme noire," *Dépêche coloniale,* June 3, 1902.

"Le Péril jaune, un document sensationnel," *Echo de Paris,* January 10, 11, 12, 1905.

Petit, Edouard. *Organisation des colonies françaises et des pays du protectorat.* 2 vols. Paris: Berger-Levrault, 1896.

Pety de Thozée, Charles. *Théories de la colonisation au XIXe siècle et la rôle de l'Etat dans le développement des colonies.* 2 vols. Brussels: Imprimerie de Hayex, 1901–2.

Peyrat, Joseph. "Le Cas de l'élite indigène dans l'Afrique du Nord," *Revue indigène* (February, 1912), 81–88.

Phillips, Edith. *The Good Quaker in French Legend.* Philadelphia: University of Pennsylvania Press, 1932.

P. H. X. [Baron d'Estournelles de Constant]. *La Politique française en Tunisie.* Paris: Librairie Plon, 1891.

Pillet, Antoine. *Des Droits de la puissance protectrice sur l'administration intérieure de l'Etat protégé.* Paris: A. Pédone, 1895.

Piolet, J. B. *La France hors de France.* Paris: Félix Alcan, 1910.

Pouvourville, Albert. *Les Défenses de l'Indo-Chine et la politique d'association.* Paris: A. Pédone, 1905.

—— "Le Maître de l'indigène," *Dépêche coloniale* (November 21, 1906).

—— "La Politique de M. Clémentel," *Dépêche coloniale* (January 5, 1906).

—— "Le Rapport Kodama et la défense de l'Indo-Chine," *Dépêche coloniale* (October 9, 1906).

Power, Thomas F. *Jules Ferry and the Renaissance of French Imperialism.* New York: King's Crown Press, 1944.

Prévost-Paradol, Lucien-Anatole. *La Nouvelle France*. Paris: Michel-Lévy Frères, 1868.

Priestley, Herbert F. *France Overseas: a Study in Modern Imperialism*. New York: D. Appleton-Century Co., 1938.

Recueil des délibérations du Congrès colonial national 1889–1890. 2 vols. Paris: Bibliothèque de "Annales économiques," 1892.

Régismanset, Charles. *Questions coloniales, 1900–1912*. Paris: E. Larose, 1912.

—— *See* Siger, Carl.

Renan, Ernest. *De l'origine du langage*. Paris: Calmann-Lévy, n.d.

Riquard, E. "Deux colonisations," *Dépêche coloniale* (June 7, 1897).

Roberts, Stephen H. *History of French Colonial Policy, 1870–1925*. 2 vols. London: King and Son, 1929.

Rolland, L., and P. Lampué. *Précis de législation coloniale*. Paris: Dalloz, 1931.

Saint-Clair, René. *L'Administrateur colonial: son rôle social et moral*. Niort: G. Clozot, 1909.

Sarraut, Albert. *Grandeur et servitude coloniales*. Paris: Editions du Sagittaire, 1931.

—— *La Mise en valeur des colonies françaises*. Paris: A. Payet, 1923.

Saussure, Léopold. *La Psychologie de la colonisation française dans ses rapports avec les sociétés indigènes*. Paris: Félix Alcan, 1899.

Seeley, J. B. *L'Expansion de l'Angleterre*. Trans. by Alfred Rambaud and Colonel Baille. Paris: A. Colin, 1885.

Seillière, Ernest. *Philosophie de l'impérialisme*. Vol. I: *Le Comte de Gobineau et l'aryanisme historique*. Paris: Librairie Plon, 1903. Vol. II: *Apollon ou Dionysos?* Paris: Librairie Plon, 1905. Vol. III: *L'Impérialisme démocratique*. Paris: Librairie Plon, 1907.

Siger, Carl [Charles Régismanset]. *Essai sur la colonisation*. 2d ed. Société de Mercure de France, 1907.

—— "Psychologie coloniale," *Mercure de France,* XXXVII (March, 1901), 793–98.

Sponck, Maurice. "Français et anglais," *Revue bleue,* VIII (July 3, 1897), 25–27.

Strachey, Sir John. *L'Inde.* Trans. by Jules Harmand. Paris: Bibliothèque générale de géographie, 1892.

Temple, Sir Richard. *L'Inde britannique.* Trans. by J. René Siefert. Paris: Nouvelle Librairie parisienne, 1889.

Terrier, Auguste. *See* Dubois, Marcel.

Thibaudet, Albert. *Les Idées politiques de la France.* Paris: Librairie Stock, 1932.

Trabant, Georges. "Association, assimilation, adaptation," *Dépêche coloniale* (September 21, 1906).

Trouillet, J. Paul. "Politique d'association," *Dépêche coloniale* (September 25, 1905).

Vaccaro, Michel-Ange. *Bases sociologiques du Droit et de l'Etat.* Trans. by J. Caure. Paris: V. Girard et E. Brière, 1898.

Valmor, G. *Les Problèmes de la colonisation.* Paris: Marcel Rivière, 1909.

Vignon, Louis. "Les Colonies françaises," extract from the *Revue britannique,* reprinted in Paris, 1885.

—— *L'Exploitation de notre empire colonial.* Paris: Hachette et Cie., 1900.

—— "La Politique du protectorat et l'inégalité des races," *Revue bleue,* III (March 25, 1905), 372–76, and (April 1, 1905), 400–403.

—— *Un Programme de politique coloniale.* Paris: Plon-Nourrit, 1919.

—— "Les Sociétés indigènes; politique qui doivent suivre à leur égard des nations colonisatrices," *Revue scientifique,* X (February 5, 1898), 161–71.

Villaumin, Robert. *See* Clozel, F. J.

Weinstein, Harold. *Jean Jaurès, a Study of Patriotism in the French Socialist Movement.* New York: Columbia University Press, 1936.

Whitehead, James L. *French Reaction to American Imperialism.* Philadelphia: University of Pennsylvania, 1943.

INDEX